The Bretwalda Guide to
SECOND WORLD WAR AIRFIELDS
in Lincolnshire

Dave Clark

First Published 2015
Text Copyright © Dave Clark 2015

Bretwalda Books
Unit 8, Fir Tree Close, Epsom,
Surrey KT17 3LD

info@BretwaldaBooks.com

www.BretwaldaBooks.com

ISBN 978-1-910440-31-5

Printed and bound in Great Britain by
Marston Book Services Ltd, Oxfordshire

Bretwalda Books Ltd

CONTENTS

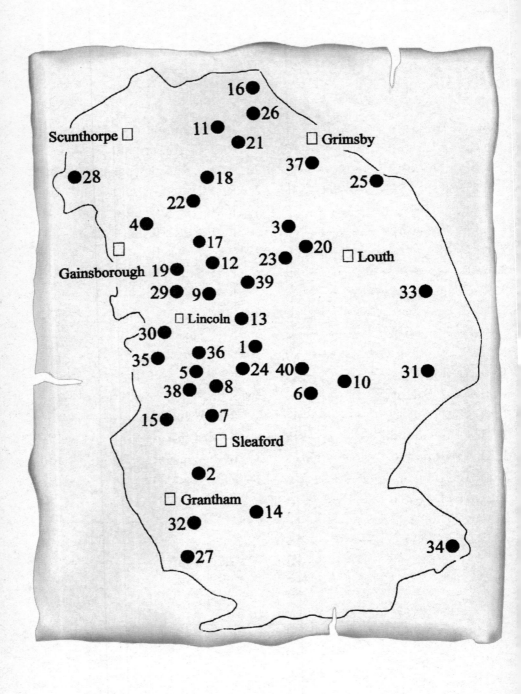

An RAF colour party and bugler attend a ceremony in 2007 at Oueilly in northern France. The many casualties of RAF Bomber Command flying from Lincolnshire are still remembered.

1. RAF BARDNEY

Location: Bardney is on the B 1190, 10 miles to the east of Horncastle. The main airfield site is to the north-east of the village.
Car Parking: Model Flying Club (Henry Lane entrance) or off-road parking on the B1202 (P).
Map: OS Explorer 273 (1471).
Refreshments: Nag's Head, Abbey Road, Bardney.

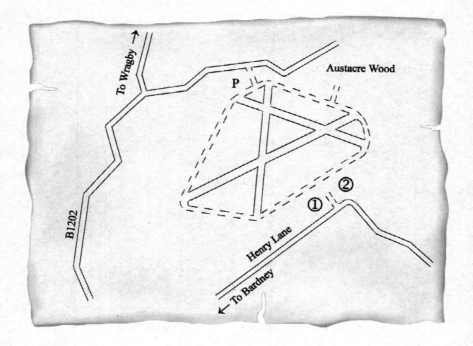

AT WAR

Group 5 Bomber Command. Operational 1943-1945. Base of No. 9 Squadron until the end of the war. No. 9 Squadron was one of only two units   617 Squadron was the other   trained to use the 'Tallboy', a 12,000lb bomb designed by Barnes Wallis. Thus, precision bombing of special 'impregnable' targets such as U-boat pens became 9 Squadron's forte. It also joined 617 Squadron in all three attacks on the battleship 'Tirpitz'. A later addition to Bardney was 189 Squadron, which included in its complement Lancaster EE136, named 'Spirit of Russia'. Built early in 1943, EE136 initially flew with 9 Squadron. With 189 Squadron, it went on to complete over one hundred operations, surviving until the 1950s.

IN PEACE

Bardney was closed to flying in October 1945. It was then used for service vehicle storage. Between 1959 and 1963, it functioned as a Thor IRBM site , after which the land reverted to mainly agricultural use. The Bardney Flyers Model Club now operate from the airfield and use the Control Tower as a clubhouse. (No 9 Squadron continues to fly, most recently serving in Afghanistan.)

RAF ground crew at a bomb dump with a selection of bombs. The choice of bombs for different raids was a skilled and complex business.

FEATURES OF INTEREST
9 Squadron Memorial, Bardney village green.
9 Squadron Standard in St. Lawrence's Church, Bardney.
Control Tower (13726/41) (1).
T2 Hangar (2).

A group of bombaimers are shown their target by an intelligence officer in 1939. At this stage of the war the RAF was over optimistic about bombing accuracy.

EXPLORATION
The perimeter track and portions of the runways survive. The northern perimeter track, with the bomb storage site in Austacre Wood is accessible via a track off the B1202 Bardney-Wragby road. The Technical Site, to the south-east, is occupied by light industrial units. The domestic sites were at the other side of Henry Lane, above North Spring Wood.

TRIVIA

All old airfields have ghost stories attached to them. Not surprisingly, perhaps, such tales usually revolve around the Control Towers. Ghostly figures and lights have long been a feature of the Coleby Grange tower. Similarly, a family living in the now demolished Elsham Wolds tower often reported eerie sightings of wartime aircrew. Bardney has two haunted spots: one in the vicinity of the Control Tower and another in Austacre Wood.

CHECK OUT

Bardney Flyers Model Club website for details of events/access.
Bardney Heritage Centre website for details of displays.
Bardney Village History website.

The propeller from a Lancaster bomber of No.9 Squadron forms the memorial marking the site of RAF Bardney.

2. RAF Barkston Heath

Location: On the B6403 (Ermine Street), 1½ miles to the south of Ancaster.
Car Parking: Heath Lane (P).
Map: OS Explorer 247 (9641).
Refreshments: The Ermine, Ancaster.

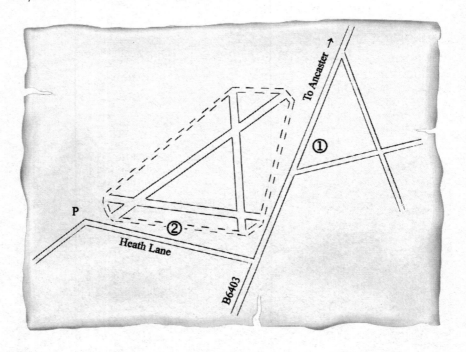

AT WAR

The site was used in the 1930s as a RLG for RAF Cranwell, opening as a station in its own right towards the end of 1942. Activity was intermittent and, following upgrading to provide hard runways, the station was allocated to the 9th USAAF. In February 1944, the 61st Troop Carrier Group arrived with Douglas Dakotas. It subsequently ferried paratroopers to France on D-Day and carried British paratroopers to Arnhem during Operation Market Garden. The Americans remained until the spring of 1945, when the station was returned to the RAF.

IN PEACE

After the war, Barkston Heath soon reprised its original supporting role for RAF Cranwell. During the 1980s, the station accommodated Bloodhound missiles, and today maintains its RLG function. For many years, it was an important centre for model aircraft flying, but permission for this activity has been withdrawn.

FEATURES OF INTEREST

Airfield Memorial (within restricted airfield site).
4 T2 hangars (1).
Control Tower 343/43 (modified) (2).

Airfields such as Barkston Heath were home to a wide range of personnel. Here the team responsible for packing parachutes poses for a photo.

The control tower of Barkston
Heath as it is today.

EXPLORATION

Remnants of the domestic sites, situated to the south of Heath Lane, have been put to agricultural use. An unusual grouping of 4 T2 hangars, opposite the main airfield site, and used for storage, is visible from the B6403. The Control Tower can be viewed from Heath Lane.

Photographed after the war, an RAF officer views the hole blasted through the massive reinforced concrete roof of the U-boat factory at Bremen by a "Grand Slam" bomb.

TRIVIA

The generosity of the 9th USAAF was legendary. The officers and men of the 61st TGC's 14th Squadron raised enough money to 'adopt' two British war orphans, who spent 30 July 1944 at RAF Barkston Heath as the squadron's guests.

CHECK OUT

RAF - Stations website for update on education centre plans.
RAF Barkston Heath Research Group website.

3. RAF Binbrook

Location: Off the Binbrook-Rothwell road (Orford Road), 1 mile to the north-west of Binbrook.
Car Parking: Brookenby Memorial (P).
Map: OS Explorer 282 (1995).
Refreshments: The Plough Inn, Binbrook.

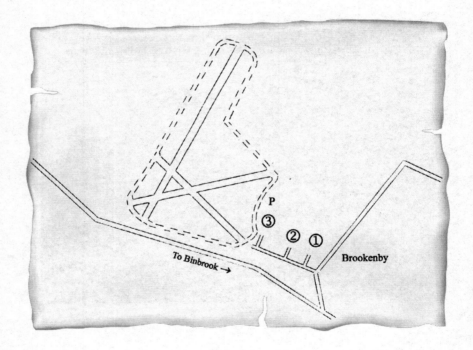

AT WAR

No. 1 Group, Bomber Command. Operational 1940-45. Initially home to 12 and 142 Squadrons, equipped first with Fairey Battles and then Wellingtons. 12 Squadron was the first to drop the 'cookie' or 'Blockbuster', a 4,000lb bomb, which the Wellingtons had to be modified to carry. The squadron was also the first to drop 'razzle', an incendiary device used to set fire to woodland (at a time when it was believed the Black Forest was being used to store armaments).

IN PEACE
Flying at Binbrook continued until 1988, Electric Canberras and, later, Lightnings, becoming a frequent sight in the skies over Lincolnshire. The station's closure led to piecemeal demolition and re-development of the facility. A community ('Brookenby') has been developed from RAF housing and a business park is centred on the Technical Site.

FEATURES OF INTEREST
Brookenby Church (Sergeants' Mess) (1).
Trading Estate site (2).
Heritage Centre, 460 (Australian) Squadron Memorial & Garden (3).
RAAF Memorial (Binbrook village).
Church of St Mary & Gabriel, Binbrook (commemorative stained glass window; RAAF Squadron 460 Roll of Honour; RAF graves in churchyard).

The old Officers' Mess was in the 1990s converted into a church dedicated to St Michael and All Angels.

15

EXPLORATION

The first turning off to the right on the Brookenby approach road leads into the village itself. Follow the signs to Brookenby Church. A little further along the approach road is the Trading Estate a treasure trove of original structures. At the top end of the approach road is the Technical Park, location of the 440 Squadron Memorial. This site is being developed as the Binbrook Heritage Centre and currently includes a small display. The RAAF Memorial in Binbrook is located on the B1203 on the left-hand side of the road as you leave the village in the direction of Market Rasen. The Market Square is a useful parking spot for both the church and The Plough Inn.

The runway at Binbrook which escaped the fate of so many wartime runways - being broken up and used as hardcore in road construction.

TRIVIA

RAF Binbrook was used as a major set in the production of the 1990 film, 'Memphis Belle'.

CHECK OUT

Binbrook Heritage Centre website.

The memorial to No.460 Squadron RAAF, an Australian unit based at Binbrook from May 1943 to June 1945.

4. RAF Blyton

Location: On the B1205, off the A159, 4½ miles to the north-east of Gainsborough. Entrance well marked.
Car Parking: Blyton Park Driving Centre (P).
Map: Ordnance Survey Explorer 280 (8795).
Refreshments: Churchill's Clubhouse or The Black Horse, Blyton.

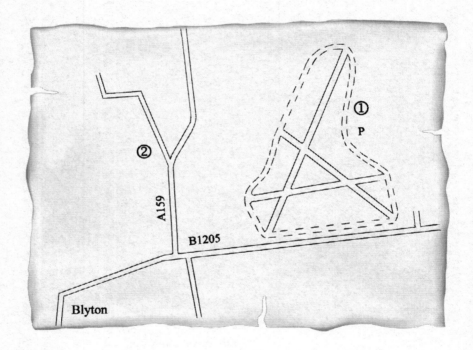

AT WAR
Group 1 Bomber Command. Operational 1942-45. Initially home to 199 Squadron. From February 1943, the station assumed a training function, with 1662 HCU schooling new crews in the skills required to fly heavy bombers a role it continued to perform until April 1945.

IN PEACE

At the end of the war, Blyton was used as a centre for receiving aircrew prior to demobilisation. In the early 1950s, it saw a brief return to prominence as a reserve USAAF base before being returned to agriculture. The remains of the runways and perimeter track are currently used for racing by Belton Park Driving Centre.

FEATURES OF INTEREST

Airfield Memorial (1).

EXPLORATION

The best time to visit is when Belton Park Driving Centre is open. The modest memorial is outside Churchill's Clubhouse. The domestic sites, of which little now survives, were grouped around the minor road to Laughton.

The bombaimer of a Vickers Wellington bomber prepares to drop his bombs in a staged photograph taken for propaganda purposes.

At a pre-mission briefing an intelligence officer points out salient features on a map to the aircrew.

TRIVIA

Airfields had their own sewage plants. Many of these, including RAF Blyton's (2), situated on the minor road to Laughton, survived the war and are in use to this day as water treatment works, serving local communities.

A squadron of Lancasters taxis forward ready to take off into the dusk ready for a nocturnal raid on Germany.

CHECK OUT

Blyton Park Driving Centre website.

The memorial at Blyton dedicated to the men who lost their lives flying from here between 1942 and 1945.

5. RAF Coleby Grange

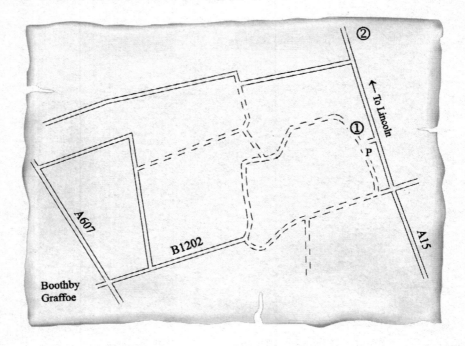

Location: Adjacent to The Kitchen restaurant/roadside café on the A15, 6 miles to the south of Lincoln.
Car Parking: The Kitchen car park (P).
Map: OS Explorer 272 (0060).
Refreshments: The Kitchen.

AT WAR

Operational 1940-44. Initially used as a Relief Landing Ground for RAF Cranwell, Fighter Command Group 12, but later assumed responsibility for Lincolnshire's night fighter defences. Squadrons in residence included 409 Squadron RCAF ('The Nighthawks') equipped with the Bristol Beaufighter and 410 Squadron RCAF, flying de Havilland Mosquitoes. The latter flew around the clock, providing home air cover during the hours of darkness, and making 'Ranger' sorties on moving targets over enemy held territory in the daytime.

IN PEACE
The airfield was closed in 1944, but operated as a Thor Missile Site between 1959 and 1963. Reverted to agricultural use soon after.

FEATURES OF INTEREST
Remains of Control Tower (pictured) (1).

The derelict control tower at RAF Coleby Grange as it stands today.

EXPLORATION

A path from the rear of the restaurant car park leads to the Control Tower. (I have always asked the restaurant proprietor for permission to walk over.) The B1202 was incorporated in the airfield perimeter track, and the points at which the track crossed and re-crossed the road are readily identifiable. The remains of the Thor Missile launching pads on Boothby Heath Farm can also be seen from the road

Michael Beetham, photographed when he was a young flight lieutenant in Lincolnshire. Beetham went on to become Chief of the Air Staff at the time of the Falklands War and to attain the rank of Marshal of the Royal Air Force.

A fuel tanker parked on an RAF station "somewhere in England" in 1942.

RAF97173

A pair of Messerschmitt Bf110. Although classed by the Germans as "destroyers", that concept was not known in Britain so they were usually described as fighters in British reports.

TRIVIA

Nearby Dunston Pillar (2) is all that remains of a 'land lighthouse', constructed in the 18th Century as a guide for travellers. In 1940, it was deemed an obstruction to aircraft coming in to land at RAF Coleby Grange, and its height was reduced by sixty feet (18.3 metres).

CHECK OUT

RCAF Squadron 409: The Nighthawks Aircrew Remembered website.

6. RAF Coningsby

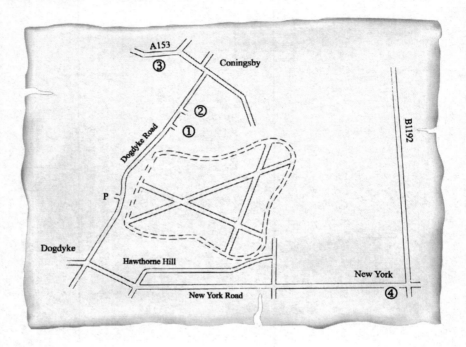

Location: In Coningsby, off the A153, 15 miles to the east of Sleaford.
Car Parking: Airfield Viewing Area, Dogdyke Road (P).
Map: OS Explorer 261 (2256).
Refreshments: Packet Inn, Dogdyke or mobile café, Viewing Area, during the summer months.

AT WAR

Group 5 Bomber Command. Operational 1941-46. Part of the pre-war airfield expansion programme. The first occupants were 97 and 106 Squadrons with Manchesters and Hampdens. In the early days, navigation techniques left a lot to be desired. For example, returning from a raid on Karlsruhe in the early hours of 2 October 1941, Pilot-Sergeant H J Newby of 106 Squadron got lost in fog. He thought he might be over Scotland. He and his crew baled out to find they were actually in Eire, a neutral country, and they were interned for the duration. Following short stints by 617 and 619 Squadrons, 83 and 97 Squadrons arrived. On the night of 21/22 June 1944, Flight-Lieutenant Ronald Walker's Lancaster of 83 Squadron was brought down over the Netherlands. His crew were killed but he survived, only to be shot by local German Security Police. Such treatment was not uncommon in the final year of the war.

IN PEACE

Squadrons 83 and 97 left Coningsby in 1946, but Bomber Command retained its presence there until 1964, with English Electric's Canberra followed by the Avro Vulcan. The station was then transferred to Fighter Command, flying Phantom, Tornado and, at the present time, Typhoon fighter jets.

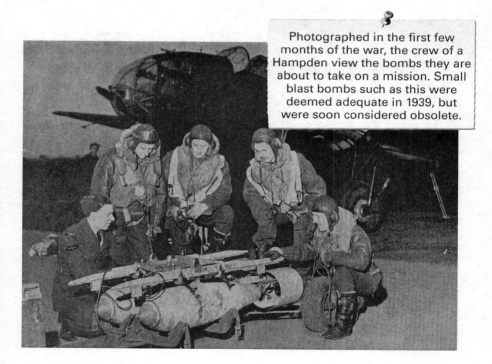

Photographed in the first few months of the war, the crew of a Hampden view the bombs they are about to take on a mission. Small blast bombs such as this were deemed adequate in 1939, but were soon considered obsolete.

The nose of a Lancaster bomber. The front gunner sat with his legs dangling down, while the bombaimer peered through the lower perspex dome.

The crews of bombers were driven to their aircraft in trucks, as here "somewhere in England".

FEATURES OF INTEREST
Battle of Britain Memorial Flight (BBMF) museum (Free) and tours of exhibits (Entry Fee) including Lancaster, Hurricane and several Spitfires (1).
Coningsby cemetery, with section dedicated to air crew (2).
Airmen's Chapel in St Michael's Church, Coningsby (3).

EXPLORATION
The runway layout has changed the main runway being lengthened during refurbishment 1954-56. A single track road at Hawthorn Hill, off New York Road, affords excellent views of the old southern portion of the airfield.

TRIVIA
At the New York end of Dogdyke Road is a line of lime trees, planted in 1995 and accompanied by a small stone bearing a plaque with the inscription: 'These limes commemorate 50 years of peace. Presented by Brymore School, Somerset' (4). The origins of this fine gesture appear to have been forgotten.

CHECK OUT
RAF BBMF website.

The modern village sign for Coningsby keeps alive the memory of the Lancaster bombers.

7. RAF Cranwell

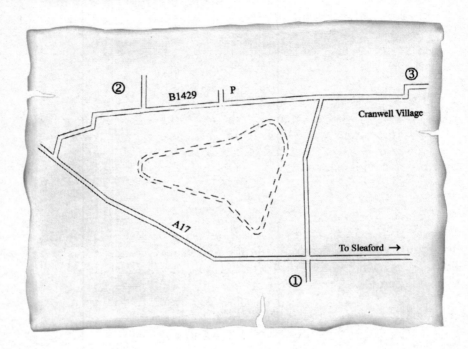

Location: On the B1429, off the A17, 3 miles to the north-west of Sleaford.

Car Parking: Aviation Heritage Centre, Heath Farm, North Rauceby/Spar, Delhi Square, Cranwell (P) and on-road parking by the church.

Map: OS Explorer 272 (0049).

Refreshments: The Bustard Inn, North Rauceby.

AT WAR

Cranwell's illustrious career as the training ground for the RAF began after the First World War, in 1920, with the establishment of the RAF Cadet College. In 1929, it was renamed the 'Royal Air Force College' which was to close at the end of August 1939, as Cranwell began to focus more keenly on preparing for war. A number of departments were moved to other locations. Even the RAF Hospital was re-located displacing the mental hospital at nearby South Rauceby. Without doubt, Cranwell's most important work during the war lay in the development of the jet fighter. On 15 May 1941, the first British jet-powered flight took place, via a Whittle jet engine installed in the Gloster 'Pioneer'. Work to develop jet fighters continued in a hangar allocated to Gloster Aircraft for this purpose. The fully-fledged Gloster Meteor jet eventually went into action in July 1944.

IN PEACE

The Royal Air Force College re-opened in 1946. Concrete runways were introduced in 1954. Remarkably, for the previous 40 years, the station had contrived to function with grass runways. Today, Cranwell continues its work in terms of the quality (if not the quantity) of trained personnel.

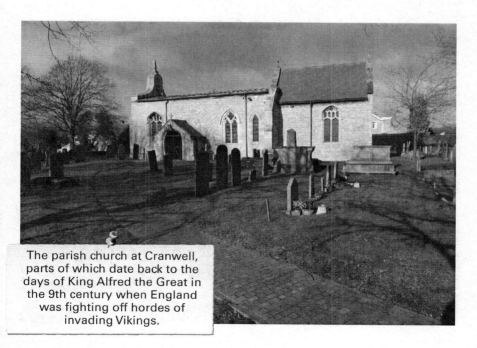

The parish church at Cranwell, parts of which date back to the days of King Alfred the Great in the 9th century when England was fighting off hordes of invading Vikings.

FEATURES OF INTEREST
Cranwell Aviation Heritage Centre (1).
RAF College (exterior) (2).
RAF graves in St. Andrew's churchyard, Cranwell village (3).

EXPLORATION
A minor road skirting the east of the main airfield site is walkable (with care) and is often used by aeroplane spotters. Good views of the RAF College and the airfield Control Tower from the B1429.

TRIVIA
RAF Cranwell had its own railway line to Sleaford. Up and running in 1918, it closed in 1956, although portions of the track bed remain in use as part of a public footpath.

A photograph showing a squadron's staff officers waiting on top of a control tower as bombers are due back from a raid.

A flight of Wellington bombers flying in tight formation in a pre-war publicity photo. Such tight formations were quickly abandoned after experience of German fighter tactics.

CHECK OUT
Cranwell Aviation Heritage Centre website.

8. RAF Digby

Location: On the B1191, off the A15, 12 miles to the south of Lincoln.
Car Parking: Commonwealth War Graves Commission cemetery, Scopwick (P) or Sports Field car park, RAF Digby, if visiting museum.
Map: OS Explorer 272 (0456).
Refreshments: The Royal Oak, Scopwick (3),

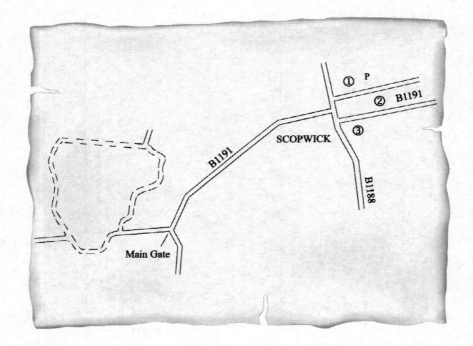

AT WAR

12 Group Fighter Command. Operational 1939-45.The station began life towards the end of World War I. Flying continued throughout the inter-war years and Digby benefited from the 1930s airfield building programme, which provided it with new hangars, administrative buildings and accommodation for personnel. Much of its early Second World War work involved off-shore North Sea patrols with Hurricanes

and Spitfires. In 1942, Digby was handed over to the Canadians, becoming RCAF Digby. Activities were wide ranging: escort duty for bombers; night patrols; roving daytime patrols; air-sea rescue work. Notable missions included RCAF 411 Squadron's role in providing air cover for the disastrous 'Dieppe Raid' (19 August 1942) in which 6,000 Canadian troops attempted to storm the heavily defended port of Dieppe. Digby was handed back to the RAF in 1945 after being associated, during the war years alone, with some fifty squadrons.

IN PEACE
Flying continued at Digby until 1953, but it remained an RAF station until 2005 when it was handed over to the Joint Service Signals Organisation.

A Spitfire stands on the ground at Digby while a formation of fighters flies overhead.

FEATURES OF INTEREST
Airfield Memorial mounted replica Spitfire & 411 Squadron Memorial (both within base).
RAF Digby Museum, with replica wartime Operations Room.
Commonwealth War Graves Commission cemetery, Scopwick (1).
Holy Cross Church, Scopwick, housing a copy of war poet John Magee's poem, 'High Flight' (2).

An air gunner being trained. Training began on static, ground mountings and then moved on to air training on older aircraft.

A staged publicity shot from 1939 shows two Hampden crews peering up into the sky in front of one of their bombers.

RAF gravestones in the churchyard of Digby's St.Thomas Martyr's church, mute testimony to the price paid by the men who flew from Lincolnshire.

EXPLORATION

Digby continues to function as a Ministry of Defence intelligence establishment. Although the main airfield site is out of bounds, the museum is open, by arrangement, at 11.00am on Sundays during the summer.

TRIVIA

Digby's Operations Centre was based at neighbouring Blankney Hall and several WAAFs lived on site. The Londsborough family, Blankney's owners, were renowned for their hospitality to Digby's service personnel. The Hall was burned to the ground in a fire that was electrical in origin and caused, it was rumoured, by a WAAF who left an iron switched on.

CHECK OUT

JSSO Digby Sector Ops Museum website.

9. RAF Dunholme Lodge

Location: To the west of the villages of Dunholme and Welton, off the A46, 5 miles from Lincoln.
Car Parking: In Welton and/or along track off minor road to Welton (P).
Map: OS Explorer 272 (0078).
Refreshments: The Black Bull, Welton.

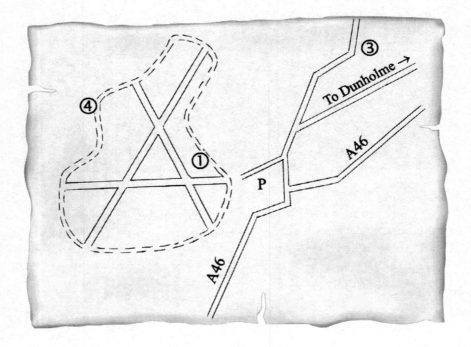

AT WAR

Group 5, Bomber Command. Operational 1943-1944. In May 1943, 44 Squadron (Rhodesia) was transferred from RAF Waddington. A year later, it was joined by 619 Squadron. On 21/22 June 1944, both units took part in a raid on a the synthetic oil factory at Wesseling.

The mission went disastrously wrong, with 44 and 619 Squadrons each losing six Lancasters. In September 1944, Dunholme Lodge was closed to flying. Albeit rather late in the day, it was considered to be too close to RAF Scampton. By this time, 44 Squadron had suffered the highest number of casualties in Group 5 and the third highest of any squadron in Bomber Command. Thereafter, until the station closed in 1945, it was used by General Aircraft Ltd for the manufacture of gliders.

IN PEACE

For a time after the war, the site was used for motor racing. (Stirling Moss and John Surtees are two of the famous names associated with the Dunholme Lodge circuit.) From 1959, the RAF was in possession once more, with the installation of 'Bloodhound' surface-to-air missiles. In 1964, the site was dismantled and returned to agricultural use.

A photo of an Avro Lancaster. This is the B1 variant, which remained in production with only minor changes from 1942 to the end of the war.

FEATURES OF INTEREST

Airfield Memorial, in grounds of Dunholme Lodge (1). Permission needed to visit.

Stained glass window (commemorating air service personnel of the First World War) in St. Mary's Church, Welton (2).

44 Squadron memorial plaque in St. Chad's Church, Dunholme.

Squadron memorials in William Farr School, Welton (3). Permission needed to visit.

Firing Range butts (4), on the public footpath leading from Green Lane (993787).

EXPLORATION

A public footpath runs across the main airfield site. Apart from the Firing Range wall, there is little left to see. The domestic sites were to the east, mainly to the south of Welton. A few structures survive.

The Black Bull pub in nearby Welton was a favourite haunt of the men from Dunholme Lodge, and is today the upstairs dining room is reputed to be haunted by the ghost of one of them.

A trio of cooks show off some of the vast amount of food that had to be cooked on a daily basis to keep a bomber station operational.

TRIVIA

The airfield runways were completed on 23 February 1943. We know this because a member of the workforce etched the date '23/2/43' in the concrete of the N-E runway. A tiny portion of the runway, including the inscription, survives.

CHECK OUT

William Farr C of E Comprehensive School website.
Lincolnshire Open Gardens website. (The garden of Dunholme Lodge opens for charity annually).

10. RAF East Kirkby

Location: On the A155, mid-way between Sleaford and Skegness.
Car Parking: Aviation Heritage Centre (P).
Map: OS Explorer 273 (3362).
Refreshments: Aviation Heritage Centre and/or Red Lion, East Kirkby.

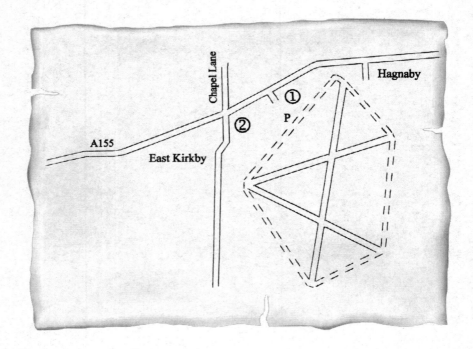

AT WAR

Group 5 Bomber Command. Operational 1943-45. Home to 57
Squadron and, later, 630 Squadron   formed from one of 57's
detachments. 57 Squadron suffered the highest casualty rate in Bomber
Command. The station's worst night was 21/22 June 1944 when
eleven of its Lancasters failed to return from a raid on Wesseling's
synthetic oil plant. In July 1945, 460 Squadron arrived with a few
Avro Lincolns in preparation for operations against Japan. Although

the Lincolns were never used for this purpose, they did go on to see some service in British colonial conflicts.

IN PEACE

After the war, the RAF retained East Kirkby on a C&M basis. During the 1950s, the USAF took it over for use as a reserve airfield. In 1964, the land was sold and returned to agricultural use. A portion of the main airfield site was subsequently developed as the East Kirkby Aviation Heritage Centre by Fred and Harold Panton, in memory of their brother, Christopher, who was killed in 1944 during a raid on Nuremberg.

The famous Lancaster bomber Just Jane taxis along the runway at East Kirkby. Just Jane is one of only three remaining Lancasters that can move under their own power.

FEATURES OF INTEREST
Aviation Heritage Centre, with Control Tower, Exhibition Hangar and much more, including Lancaster NX611, 'Just Jane'. (Entry Fee). Airfield Memorial (1) (Aviation Heritage Centre entrance).

EXPLORATION
The Hagnaby-Stickford road (portions of which correspond to the perimeter track) crosses one of the subsidiary runways, lengthened by the USAF during its post-war occupation. The domestic sites were centred on Chapel Lane, to the north. A scattering of maycrete buildings survive.

TRIVIA
The Red Lion (2) was the watering-hole for East Kirkby's aircrews. It was not an unusual occurrence for them to slip under the security fence and pop in for a pint without recourse to checking in and out of the main gate.

On the days when the Lancaster Just Jane is powered up and taxis around East Kirkby it takes paying passengers.

CHECK OUT
Lincolnshire Aviation Heritage Centre website.

The monument to 55 Base, the HQ for RAF Spilsby, RAF Strubby and RAF East Kirkby. After the dedication, the monument was overflown by the Battle of Britain Memorial Flight's Lancaster captained by Mike Chatterton, watched by his father John, who flew from East Kirkby.

11. RAF Elsham Wolds

Location: On the A15, 5 miles south of Barton-Upon-Humber.
Car Parking: Anglian Water Treatment Works (for the memorial) (P).
Map: OS Explorer 281 (0413).
Refreshments: Whistle & Flute, Barnetby le Wold.

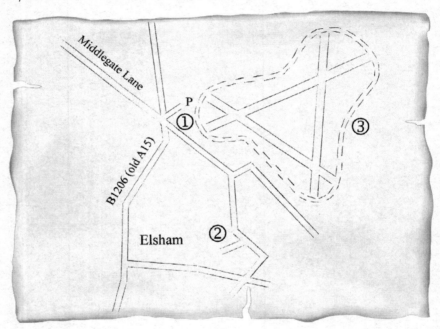

AT WAR

No. 1 Group Bomber Command. Operational 1941-45. Primarily home to 103 Squadron and to aircraft ED888, the longest-serving active Lancaster in Bomber Command. By the end of 1944, ED888, or 'Mike Squared' as it was known, had completed its 140th mission. 103 Squadron crews flew practically everything, starting with the Fairey Battle, then the Vickers Wellington followed by the Handley Page Halifax and, finally, the Avro Lancaster Mark III.

IN PEACE

Elsham Wolds closed in the late 1940s, following a period when it was used by gliders. Initially, the land returned to agriculture, but a dual carriageway (A15) now passes through the main airfield site, following the course of the N-S runway. An industrial estate has been developed on the road's eastern flank.

FEATURES OF INTEREST

Airfield Memorial & Garden (Anglian Water Treatment Works) (1).
Memorial Rooms (within Anglian Water Treatment Works building).
Squadron Memorial in All Saints Church, Elsham (2).
J Type hangar (3).

The J-Type hangar that survives at Elsham Wolds. This type of hangar was designed to have a useable working space measuring 150 by 300 feet - big enough for the largest bombers.

EXPLORATION

The domestic sites were situated to the south-east. A few remains can be seen off the lower reaches of Middlegate Road. For the church, there is a little rough off-road parking by the woods. The J Type hangar can be reached via the industrial estate junction off the A15 dual-carriageway. It stands in splendid isolation on the JHP site.

TRIVIA

Elsham was the site for one of twenty airfields that were located in Lincolnshire during the First World War. Operational between 1916 and 1919, the station was home to 33 Squadron which defended the coast against Zeppelin raids. The small airfield was immediately to the north-east of the present-day industrial estate.

Pilot Officer R.R. Reed and his crew inspect battle damage on their aircraft.

CHECK OUT
Tiny Purple Grapes All Saints, Elsham website for details of church and Memorial Rooms opening times.

Pilot Officer E.T. Jones and Flying Officer E.N. Hooke peer out through a hole torn in the side of their bomber by fire from an enemy fighter.

A photo of the men of No.103 Squadron taken at Elsham Wolds in August 1942.

49

12. RAF Faldingworth

Location: On the minor road between Faldingworth and Spridlington, linking the A15 with the A46. Follow sign to Newtoft Business Park.
Car Parking: By Memorial (P).
Map: OS Explorer 272 (0385).
Refreshments: Coach & Horses, Faldingworth.

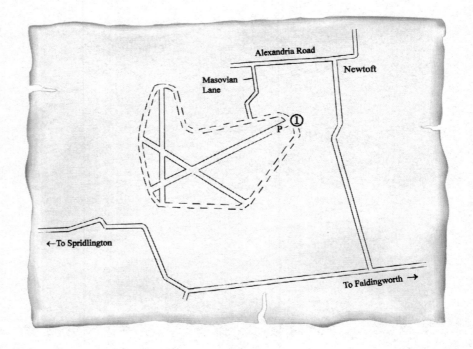

AT WAR

1 Group Bomber Command. Operational 1943-46. Initially used as a base for 1667 Heavy Conversion Unit, but most closely associated with 300 (Masovian) Squadron, which arrived from RAF Ingham in March 1944. This was Bomber Command's first Polish squadron and it remained at Faldingworth until it disbanded in 1946. Casualties

mounted steadily and, in common with other Polish squadrons, losses had to be made good by the addition of non-Polish crews.

IN PEACE
Appropriately, perhaps, RAF Faldingworth finished the war as a holding camp for Polish forces. In the 1950s, it was used for the storage of nuclear weapons. During the 1970s, it was taken over by an armaments manufacturer for weapons testing. Much of the main airfield site has since been returned to agricultural use, but the south-west corner is still given over to industry.

FEATURES OF INTEREST
Airfield Memorial (1)
All Saints Church, Faldingworth (includes stained glass window; memorial plaque; memorial porch gates; 'Path of Friendship').
Memorabilia in Coach & Horses, Faldingworth.

A Hampden bomber, one of 1,430 built for the RAF between 1938 and 1941. The bomber was withdrawn from frontline service in 1942.

EXPLORATION

Domestic sites were to the north of the main airfield site. Some structures remain. For the memorial, approach via Alexandria Road, Newtoft ('Middle Farm' on OS Explorer 272) and Masovian Lane. The entrance is gated   usually open, but with a notice giving details of keyholders. Follow the track in and bear left through Newton Covert. Another left turn onto the perimeter track takes you to the main Memorial, flanked by a row of small memorials to individuals. The runways and perimeter track (in very poor repair) are largely intact. During the week, explosives testing can be heard from the southern portion of the airfield. A few post-war accommodation blocks can be seen by following Alexandria Road down to the end. The 'Path of Friendship' at the church relates to the new paved walkway. Look out for the handshake symbol near the door. (There is a little on-road parking by the telephone kiosk).

A group of trainee navigators inspect a target map. The long, thin map shows the approach to a target with key features that the navigators were expected to spot from the air.

The memorial at RAF Faldingworth, made out of undressed slabs of local stone.

TRIVIA

Lincolnshire's bomber airfields, with perhaps 2,000 personnel, often dwarfed the local villages after which they were named. They had their own churches, post offices, shops and cinemas. The cinema buildings at RAF Wickenby and RAF Faldingworth are among those that have survived. The latter is shown on OS Explorer 272, standing on its own between Dogland Farm and a surviving B1 hangar.

CHECK OUT

Faldingworth Memorials website.

13. RAF Fiskerton

Location: 4 miles to the east of Lincoln, off the A158.
Car Parking: Airfield Memorial (P).
Map: Ordnance Survey Explorer 272 (0572).
Refreshments: Carpenters Arms, Fiskerton.

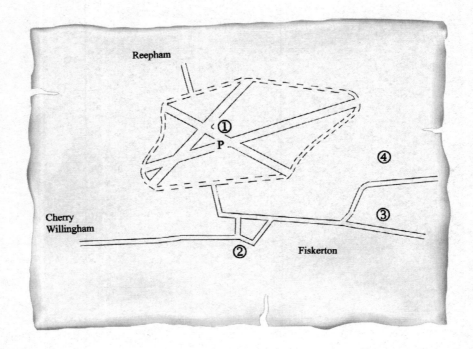

AT WAR

Group 5 Bomber Command. Operational 1943-45. Initially home to 49 Squadron. Early missions included a raid on the largest gas holder in Europe, at Oberhausen (14/15 June 1943). In September 1943, the runways were closed for resurfacing. They had begun to show signs of fatigue at an early stage and continued to pose problems throughout the war. The night of 21/22 June 1944 was Fiskerton's costliest of the war. 49 Squadron contributed twenty Lancasters to a raid on

Wesseling's synthetic oil plant and lost six aircraft. In October 1944, 49 Squadron moved to RAF Fulbeck to be replaced by 576 Squadron, which would eventually (25 April 1945) participate in an unusual daylight raid, aimed at the SS barracks at Berchtesgaden. Air crews were told to feel free to bomb the 'Berghof' if they found the Fuhrer at home.

IN PEACE

The station was closed to flying in October 1945, but between 1960 and 1992, it played a significant civil defence role as one of the Royal Observer Corps' Protected Group Control Centres, geared to monitoring fallout in the event of a nuclear war. Land use is now split between farming and industry. Portions of the runways and perimeter track have survived. The ROC site is occupied by 'Primetake', which manufactures ammunition. The firm has incorporated the wartime firing range butts (along the Moor Lane bridleway) in its testing ground.

The monument at RAF Fiskerton which stands close to the old main runway.

A scene inside the control tower at Fiskerton.

FEATURES OF INTEREST
Airfield Memorial (1).
Memorial plaques to Squadrons 49 and 576 in St. Clement's Church, Fiskerton (2).
Remains of Communal Sites No 3 (3) (Tanya wool factory) and No 4 (Hall Farm) (4).

EXPLORATION
Public footpaths traverse the main airfield site. The Fiskerton-Reepham road (now reinstated) was closed when the airfield was constructed.

TRIVIA
In 1997, reserves of oil were discovered beneath the main airfield site. An unobtrusive drilling operation is conducted by Cirque Energy.

CHECK OUT
RAF Fiskerton website.

E.L. Saslove of No.576 Squadron photographed during his service at Fiskerton. Saslove was killed on a raid to Munich after he held his stricken bomber steady while his crew baled out.

The ground crew of a Lancaster belonging to No.576 Squadron at Fiskerton.

14. RAF/USAAF Folkingham

Location: Near Aslackby 10 miles to the south of Sleaford. Leave the A15 at Aslackby and follow the road through the village. It comes to an end at the gated entrance to the main airfield site.
Car Parking: Temple Wood (P).
Map: OS Explorer 248 (0429).

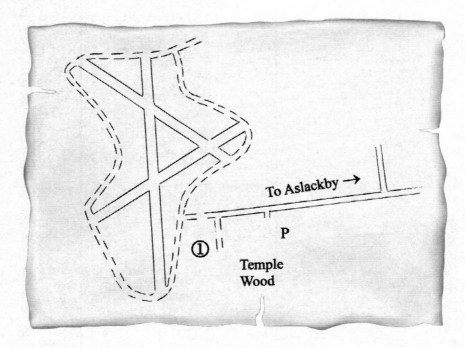

Refreshments: New Inn, West Street, Folkingham.

AT WAR

American 9th Army Air Force. Operational 1944-45. The site had been active since 1940, when it was developed as a dummy airfield to divert the attention of the Luftwaffe from RAF Spittlegate. In 1943, it was upgraded and handed over to the 313th TCG USAAF in February

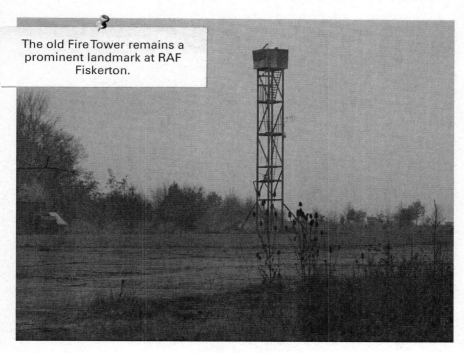

The old Fire Tower remains a prominent landmark at RAF Fiskerton.

1944, to help prepare for the D-Day landings. Accordingly, on 6 June 1944, Douglas Dakota C-47s ferried paratroopers to a drop zone at Picauville. Between 17 and 29 September 1944, men, vehicles and supplies were flown to Arnhem in support of the doomed 'Operation Market Garden'. In March 1945, the 313th moved to a new forward base at Achiet in France, and Folkingham was handed back to the RAF. The station was closed in 1946.

IN PEACE

After the war, the racing driver, Raymond Mays used the airfield as a testing ground for BRM. Between 1959 and 1963, Folkingham served as a Thor Missile base, in the care of 223 Squadron. BRM returned for a while, but the southern portion of the airfield was soon returned to agricultural use, while the northern portion became a scrap yard for military/commercial vehicles and machinery.

Robert Saundby (centre) and Sir Richard Peirse inspect a map at RAF Bomber Command HQ before issuing orders for a bombing mission.

FEATURES OF INTEREST
Airfield Memorial in cemetery off Temple Road, Aslackby.

EXPLORATION
Difficult. The public footpath system is fragmented and the main airfield site is out of bounds. Evidence of the bomb storage site (1) can be seen in Temple Wood. The remains of the Thor Missile launching pads can be seen to the right, as you stand at the end of the road from Aslackby. The domestic sites were located in the fields beyond, towards Folkingham. A truncated bridleway to the north of Kilsby leads to the surviving Firing Range wall.

TRIVIA
BRM was based locally in Bourne and Folkingham appeared to be ideally situated to provide a home for British motor racing. It was not to be, the prize eventually going to another Second World Airfield: Silverstone in Northamptonshire.

CHECK OUT
War History Online website for photographs/details of scrapped military vehicles at Folkingham.

The memorial at RAF Folkingham.

A marine mine being loaded on to a Hampden bomber. The Hampden flying from Lincolnshire was widely used for laying mines and other marine duties in the early years of the war.

15. RAF/USAAF Fulbeck

Location: 10 miles to the east of Newark, off the A17, on the minor road to Stragglethorpe.
Car Parking: By Memorial, main entrance (P).
Map: OS Explorer 271 (8950) & 272 (9051).
Refreshment: The Hare & Hounds, Fulbeck.

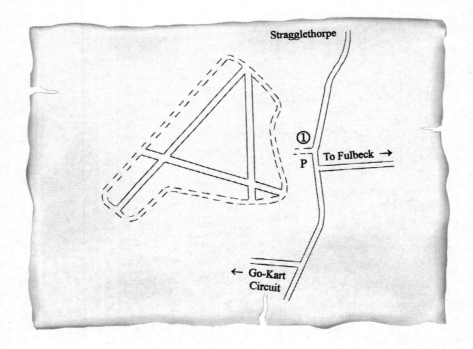

AT WAR

Operational 1940-45. Initially, Fulbeck served as a RLG for RAF Cranwell. During 1942, hard runways were constructed and on 1 October 1943, the station was handed over to the United States 9th Army Air Force. The 442nd Troop Carrier Group, equipped with Douglas C-47 Dakotas, participated in the D-Day landings, transporting the 82nd Airborne Division to its drop zone near St. Mere

Eglise. In August 1944, the 440th took over to continue support operations, and went on to ferry field-artillery to Nijmegen as part of 'Operation Market Garden'. Many of the C-47s, heavy and slow, were shot down. Soon after, the Americans moved out and Fulbeck was returned to RAF 5 Group Bomber Command, with Squadrons 49 and 189. During the spring of 1945, both squadrons took part in several important raids on oil installations.

IN PEACE

Fulbeck ended its flying life as it had begun, operating as a RLG for RAF Cranwell until 1970. It was then returned to agriculture. Portions of the site are still used for occasional army manoeuvres, while other parts are used for go-karting. It has successfully fended off an application for use as a nuclear waste dump, but is currently threatened by wind farm development.

A German Folke Wulf FW190 fighter, an awesomely effective opponent of the RAF after it was introduced in 1941.

The main railway station in Berlin, photographed in 1945. The German rail network was a primary target for Bomber Command throughout the war.

FEATURES OF INTEREST
Airfield Memorial (1).
Memorial rose in St Nicholas's churchyard, Fulbeck.

EXPLORATION
A public bridleway servicing the PFI kart circuit skirts the southern portion of the main airfield site. The domestic sites, of which evidence can be seen, were dispersed to the east, off the minor road to Fulbeck. During the war, Fulbeck Hall was occupied by the Americans. A small, privately owned museum in commemoration of the Arnhem campaign is established here.

TRIVIA

During the St. Mere Eglise drop, Private John Steele's parachute got caught in the town church spire, and he remained suspended there while the fight for the town continued. The incident was later portrayed in the film 'The Longest Day'.

CHECK OUT

Historic Houses Association website for details of access to Fulbeck Hall.

The memorial at Fulbeck. Although not clear here the upright stone slab stands on a base shaped to resemble an aircraft propeller.

16. RAF/USAAF Goxhill

Location: Focused on Goxhill village, off the A1077 10 miles to the north of Immingham.

Car Parking: Off-road parking opposite the airfield memorial on Horsegate Field Road (P).

Map: OS Explorer 284 (1121).

Refreshments: The Brocklesby Hunt, Howe Lane, Goxhill. (Has been temporarily closed. Alternatively, try Thornton Hunt Inn at nearby Thornton Curtis.)

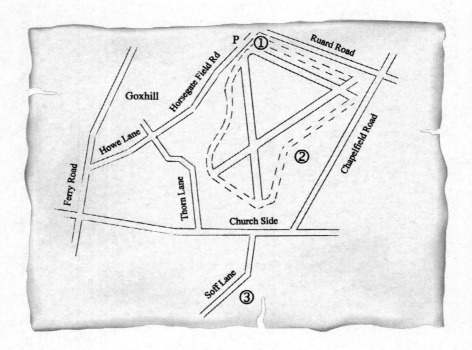

AT WAR

Operational 1941-1945. Initially used by the RAF as a base for target-towing practice. Goxhill was the first RAF base to be taken over by the

A P-38 Lightning fighter photographed at Goxhill. The P-38 was used most in the Pacific theatre where its long range was made it invaluable.

Americans. In June 1942, General Eisenhower attended a special ceremony to mark the occasion. In the hands of the USAAF 8th Air Force, Goxhill was used as a base for the training of pilots for the Lockheed P-38 'Lightning' fighter. The young Americans enjoyed taking risks and there were more than 50 crashes, resulting in 23 deaths. In January 1945, the airfield was handed back to RAF Fighter Command before being passed to Maintenance Command for bomb storage.

IN PEACE

The land was sold off piecemeal during the 1960s and 1970s. The airfield itself reverted to agriculture and although the tarmac has gone, the runways as discernible as rough grass tracks. A number of ancillary sites have survived, and many of the wartime single-storey buildings are being developed as light industrial units.

Sir Arthur "Bomber" Harris (right)
at his desk in the HQ of RAF
Bomber Command. It was Harris
who brought Bomber Command
to its peak of effectiveness.

FEATURES OF INTEREST
Airfield memorial with information panel (1).
Technical Site including a J Type hangar, capable of accommodating the largest of wartime aircraft and two T2 hangars (2).
Soff Lane Domestic Site (3)

EXPLORATION
A public footpath leading from Trinity Close crosses the main airfield site, facilitating a circular walk, taking in the Technical Site and Soff Lane Domestic Site.

TRIVIA

Goxhill's Control Tower survived until 2003, when it was dismantled and shipped to America where it was reassembled. It is now exhibited in the Military Aviation Museum, Virginia.

CHECK OUT

Airfield Archaeology website contains a well-illustrated feature on RAF/USAAF Goxhill.

The monument at RAF Goxhill, which features a propeller blade taken from a crashed P-38.

17. RAF Grantham

Location: On Somerby Hill (A52), Grantham.
Car Parking: Layby on A52 (southbound) near Driver Standards Agency (P).
Map: OS Explorer 247 (9334).
Refreshments: The Fox & Hounds, Old Somersby.

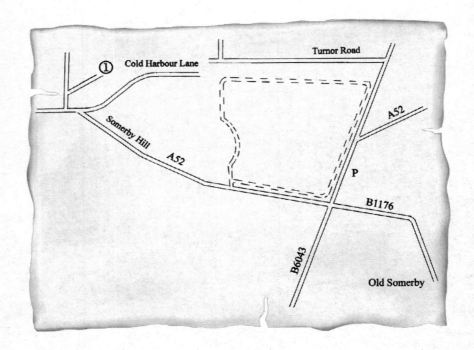

AT WAR

Flying began here during the First World War and continued throughout the inter-war years. The station's main contribution to the Second World War was as an Advanced Flying Unit between 1942 and 1945. The AFUs catered for air crew arriving from the British Empire, who lacked familiarity with British weather conditions. Much of the training took place in the twin-engine Airspeed Oxford, which remained in service with the RAF well into the 1950s. Despite its long service, the airfield never possessed hard runways.

IN PEACE

Flying continued at Grantham until the late 1940s, after which the station was used for several non-flying training purposes. In 1975, it was handed over to the army, and now functions as Prince William of Gloucester TA barracks. The eastern portion of the site is occupied by the Driver Standards Agency.

After being given their briefing for a mission, navigators study maps of the route to familiarise themselves with landmarks and enemy danger spots.

An Airspeed Oxford photographed at Grantham. This versatile trainer was produced in large numbers and more than 11 variants for different purposes.

FEATURES OF INTEREST

St. Vincent's Hall, 5 Group Bomber Command HQ (1).
Officer's Mess, dating from 1920s (shaped like a wing-nut on OS Explorer 247 and within main barracks site).

EXPLORATION

St. Vincent's Hall is now a private house (gated) at the top of St. Vincent's Road. A glimpse can also be caught to the rear of the high brick wall on Cold Harbour Lane. It is possible to do a circular walk, taking in Somerby Hill and Cold Harbour Lane, which links up with the byway, Turnor Road, off the B6403. Turnor Road (fronted with a little off-road parking) formed the northern perimeter of the airfield and, as such, has surviving pillboxes to the south of the hedgerow.

TRIVIA

It was not unusual for an RAF station's name to be changed. RAF Digby was originally RAF Scopwick, while RAF Ingham became RAF Cammeringham shortly before its closure. Also late in the day (1944), RAF Grantham became RAF Spitalgate a title derived from the old Spittlegate (Hospital Gate) area of the town.

CHECK OUT

Grantham Museum website. The area's aviation heritage is sometimes reflected in artefacts on display.

A tail gunner in his perspex-covered turret. German fighters frequently sought to kill the tail gunner first, as this would make subsequent attacks safer for them.

A pill box built to protect RAF Grantham from an attack by German paratroops.

18. RAF Grimsby/Waltham

Location: Between Waltham and Holton le Clay, off the A16, 4 miles to the south of Grimsby.
Car Parking: Waltham Windmill and Lay-by on A16 (Louth Road).
Map: OS Explorer 284 (2702).
Refreshments: Waltham Windmill and/or The Jug & Bottle, Holton le Clay.

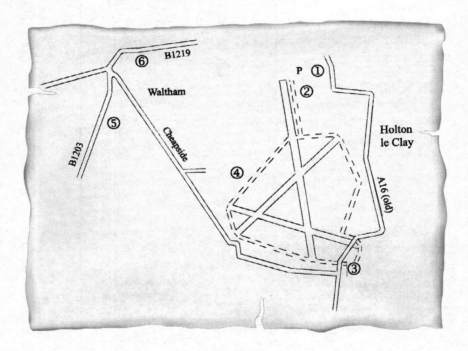

AT WAR

1 Group Bomber Command. Operational 1941-45. Initially home to 142 Squadron which lost five out of fifteen Wellingtons in a raid on aircraft factories in Kassel on 27/28 August 1942. Replaced by 100 Squadron which arrived in December 1942 and stayed until the end of the war. Lancaster bomber EE139, fresh off the production line, was

delivered at the same time and became famous as 'Phantom of the Ruhr', accumulating 121 operational flights, including missions to Berlin, Nuremberg and Peenemunde.

IN PEACE

With the departure of 100 Squadron, flying ceased and the station was used for storage. Light aircraft utilised the runways in the 1950s, but efforts to develop civil flying did not come to fruition. The Technical Site is now given over to industrial use, while go-karting activities and a golf driving range are established in the south-east corner. The Holton le Clay A16 bypass has encroached upon the eastern perimeter.

The old dilapidated control tower of RAF Grimsby.

FEATURES OF INTEREST
Airfield Memorial (1).
B1 hangar (2).
The Jug & Bottle (3).
Control Tower (Type B 7345/41) (4).
Waltham Windmill Museum (with RAF section) (5).
All Saints Church, Waltham (6).

EXPLORATION
An airfield where (surprisingly, perhaps) it is easy to spend a day. The memorial is situated in a fenced-off area at the northern end (northbound carriageway) of the A16 Holton le Clay bypass. The entrance is just beyond the traffic lights. To the rear is the B1 hangar (another useful point of reference.) The industrial estate, with plenty of parking space, is on Cheapside Road. (The public footpath system is a little more extensive than that shown on OS Explorer 284, and it is possible to walk over from the memorial site.) The Control Tower is the white building tucked away at the rear. The Waltham Logistics site leading to it is gated. If the gate is closed, walk round the perimeter fence (via the driving school barrier) and you can enter via a marked public footpath on the left. The church and museum (with parking) are both on the B1219, the main road through Waltham.

The surviving B1 Hangar with part of the extensive surviving taxi ways at RAF Grimsby.

The memorial sign that marks
the entrance to the old station
from Holton le Clay.

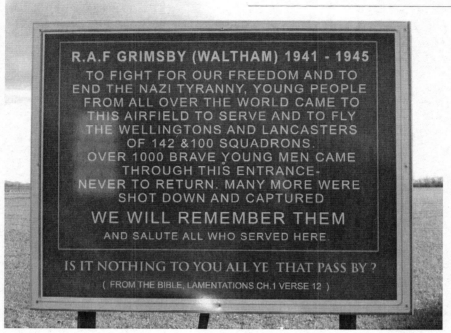

R.A.F GRIMSBY (WALTHAM) 1941 - 1945
TO FIGHT FOR OUR FREEDOM AND TO
END THE NAZI TYRANNY, YOUNG PEOPLE
FROM ALL OVER THE WORLD CAME TO
THIS AIRFIELD TO SERVE AND TO FLY
THE WELLINGTONS AND LANCASTERS
OF 142 & 100 SQUADRONS.
OVER 1000 BRAVE YOUNG MEN CAME
THROUGH THIS ENTRANCE-
NEVER TO RETURN. MANY MORE WERE
SHOT DOWN AND CAPTURED
WE WILL REMEMBER THEM
AND SALUTE ALL WHO SERVED HERE.
IS IT NOTHING TO YOU ALL YE THAT PASS BY ?
(FROM THE BIBLE, LAMENTATIONS CH.1 VERSE 12)

TRIVIA
The Jug & Bottle is named after a Lancaster bomber (PA177) of 100
Squadron, operating from RAF Grimsby. Allegedly, the aircraft's
parking spot was on the site now occupied by the pub.

CHECK OUT
Waltham Windmill website for details of museum opening times.

19. RAF Hemswell

Location: On the A631, near Caenby Corner, 8 miles to the east of Gainsborough.
Car Parking: Use Parade Ground car park off Gibson Road (P).
Map: OS Explorer 281 (9490).
Refreshments: Several cafés on-site.

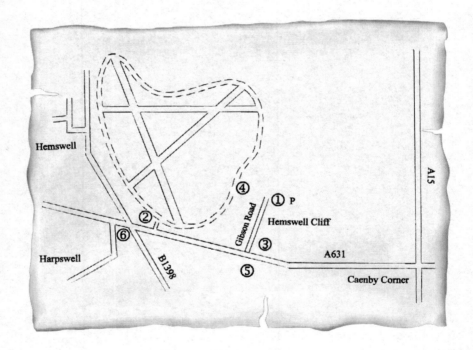

AT WAR
Group 1/Group 5 Bomber Command. Operational 1937-1945. Hemswell formed part of the airfield expansion programme of the 1930s. Its first residents were 61 and 144 Squadrons. The latter suffered 100% casualties on 29 September 1939 when five Hampdens set out to search the Heligoland area for German warships. They ran into enemy fighters and all were shot down. 144 Squadron participated

in Bomber Command's first attack on German soil   a token raid on the seaplane base at Hornum, on the island of Sylt. Polish Squadrons 300, 301 and 305 spent some time at the base in 1942/43. The last Lancaster squadron in residence (1944-45) was 170.

IN PEACE

Flying continued after the war, with the Mosquito in the late 1940s and the Avro Lincoln in the 1950s. The station became a Thor Missile base in the early years of the next decade before closing in 1967. In 1972, the facility was used to house Asians expelled from Uganda. More recently, the village of Hemswell Cliff has developed out of a portion of the main airfield site and the wartime domestic sites to the south. The remainder of the Technical Site is now given over to a mix of light industry and retail use   notably the sale of antiques.

One of several surviving hangars at Hemswell that have now been converted to use for light industrial purposes.

A bomb goes off at RAF Hemswell during the Second World War.

FEATURES OF INTEREST

Two Airfield Memorials (1), (2) & Squadron Memorial (3).
Control Tower (4).
3 C Type hangars.
Officers' Mess (Hemswell Court hotel) (5).
Station HQ (Blenheim Care Centre).
Water Tower.
Roll of Honour, St. Chad's Church, Harpswell (6).

EXPLORATION

Approaching from Caenby Corner, use the Hemswell Centres entrance. Follow Gibson Road, the main route through the complex. The Parade Ground car park is opposite Canberra Antiques. The 170 Squadron Memorial is by the entrance on the main road, near the bus stop. One Airfield Memorial is on the Parade Ground. The second, erected by the Airfields Conservation Trust, is by the entrance to the hangar area, a little further along the A631. The site is very busy on Sundays, with

The memorial to No.170 Squadron that stands at Hemswell.

car-boot sales, an indoor market (in one of the hangars) and modest car parking charges. During the week, parking is free and the atmosphere more relaxed. For the Control Tower (Quest-eeze premises), use the hangar entrance. One of the original 4 C Type hangars was destroyed by fire and an on-site RAF museum, marked on OS Explorer 281, has closed. Many of the remaining structures are clearly in need of basic maintenance.

The old water tower at Hemswell.

TRIVIA

RAF Hemswell was used for ground shots (in the role of RAF Scampton) in the 1954 feature film, 'The Dambusters'.

CHECK OUT

Hemswell Antique Centres website.

20. RAF Hibaldstow

Location: On the B1206 (the old A15), 5 miles to the south of Brigg.
Car Parking: By Memorial (P)/The Red Lion, Redbourne/Sky Dive car parking area.
Map: OS Explorer 281 (9895).
Refreshments: The Red Lion, Redbourne/Sky Dive café/restaurant.

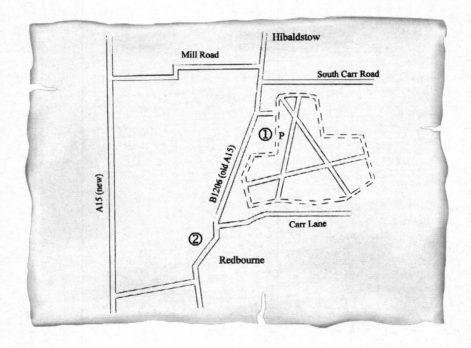

AT WAR

Group 12 Fighter Command. Operational 1941-45. The original intention was for Hibaldstow to function as a Bomber Command airfield hence the concrete runways. However, it quickly assumed a night-fighter role with 253 Squadron, equipped with Hawker Hurricanes. The hurricanes worked in tandem with 1459 Flight (later 538 Squadron) which flew Douglas Havoc fighters, each fitted with a

The monument with its accompanying flagpole beside remaining buildings at Hibaldstow.

'Turbinlite' or searchlight. The searchlight would illuminate enemy aircraft for the accompanying Hurricanes to shoot down. The station is famous for an incident that occurred in the spring of 1943 when a Spitfire took off with a mechanic clinging to its tail. Ground crew occasionally had to ride the tail while a Spitfire was taxiing in order provide stability. Following a lap of the airfield at 800 feet, pilot and mechanic landed safely. (The Spitfire concern, AB910, is still flying at RAF Coningsby, as part of the BBMF.)

IN PEACE

Flying continued until 1947, with the accommodation of an Advanced Flying Unit. The land was eventually returned to agriculture in the 1960s. Today, in addition to serving as a venue for model aircraft flying, Hibaldstow is a centre for skydiving, and in 2014, hosted the European Skydiving League Finals.

Photographed in 1940 this scene shows the Duty Officer of a bomber base waiting for news from his aircraft during a raid over Germany.

FEATURES OF INTEREST

Airfield Memorial & Information Panel (1).
Control Tower (private house), adjacent to Memorial.
The Red Lion has contemporary photographs on display (2).

EXPLORATION

The runways and perimeter track are intact. Domestic sites were to the south of the main airfield site and the area may be viewed via the minor road/public footpath network. The memorial can be approached from the track leading to Field House Farm. Note 'No Parking' signs immediately in front of the memorial, which is adjacent to the Control Tower. The Sky Dive entrance is along the single-track road (South Carr Road) leading to Hibaldstow Bridge. There are Information Panels at the memorial, at the entrance to Field House Farm and at The Red Lion.

TRIVIA

1459 Flight's C.O. was Squadron Leader James Brindley Nicholson, who had won the Victoria Cross in 1940, in the Battle of Britain. During the Second World War, a total of 23 VCs were awarded to Bomber Command aircrew. Remarkably, Nicholson was Fighter Command's only recipient.

CHECK OUT

Sky Dive Hibaldstow website for news of events and open days.
Hibaldstow Model Flying Club website.

Initial pilot training in the early years of the war saw volunteers taken up in biplane trainers.

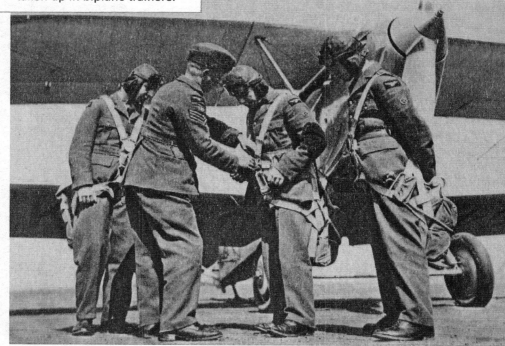

21. RAF Ingham

Location: The airfield lies on the B 1398 between the A15 and the village of Ingham, 7 miles to the north of Lincoln.
Car Parking: Off-road parking on Ingham Lane, by the weather station (P).
Map: OS Explorer 272 (9683).
Refreshments: The Windmill inn.

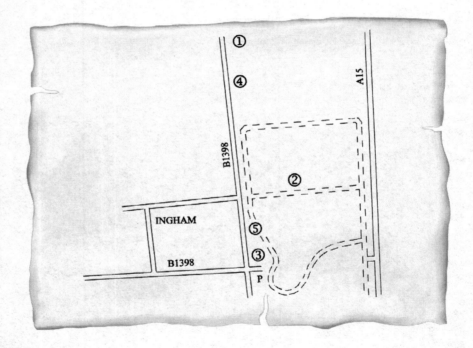

IN WAR

No 1 Group, Bomber Command. Operational 1942-45. Opened in May 1942 as a satellite of RAF Hemswell. For most of its operational life, Ingham was home to Polish squadrons, notably 300 Squadron, flying Vickers Wellingtons. Although 300 Squadron contributed to general bombing raids, it came to specialise in mine-laying operations, initially off the Friesian Islands. It was regarded as a thankless chore and the Poles hated it. The commitment of the Poles in the air could not be faulted, and their losses mounted to such an extent that British personnel had to be added to their ranks. In March 1944, the Wellingtons were replaced with Lancasters which needed concrete runways, and 300 Squadron was moved to RAF Faldingworth.

AT PEACE

Although flying at Ingham ceased before the end of the war, the station retained its Polish connection for a further three years. The Polish Air Force Film Unit was based here and, until its closure in 1948, Ingham was used as a regional centre for Polish resettlement. The land then reverted to agriculture.

FEATURES OF INTEREST

Heritage Centre (1) (Opening 2015).
Control Tower (2) (private house).
Technical Site (3).
Hare's Wood Communal Site (4) to the north and WAAF site, beyond.

A Vickers Wellington photographed at RAF Ingham. the presence of the Nash & Thompson gun turrets shows this to be a Wellington 1A.

EXPLORATION

A public footpath runs across the airfield, past Cliff House, used as an officer's mess during the war. The Control Tower (almost unrecognisable following conversion) is to the rear on private land. RAF Ingham Heritage Centre, scheduled to open in 2015, will provide a focus (and car parking) for visitors. Additional domestic sites were laid out between the E-W section of the B1398 and Ingham village.

TRIVIA

The Wellington bomber was designed to take tremendous punishment. During a raid on Bremen on 4/5 September 1943, one of 300 Squadron's Wellingtons lost most of its fuselage cover and still made it home. A photograph of this particular aircraft can be seen in The Windmill inn (5).

CHECK OUT

RAF Ingham Heritage Group website.

The overgrown escape hatch from one of the deep bomb shelters at RAF Ingham.

The remaining barrack buildings, just some of several structures to remain at Ingham.

The interior of one of the bomb shelters at Ingham.

22. RAF Kelstern

Location: To the north-east of the hamlet of Kelstern, which is off the A631, 5 miles to the west of Louth.
Car Parking: Off road parking by the Operations Block (P).
Map: OS Explorer 282 (2691).
Refreshments: Plough Inn, Binbrook

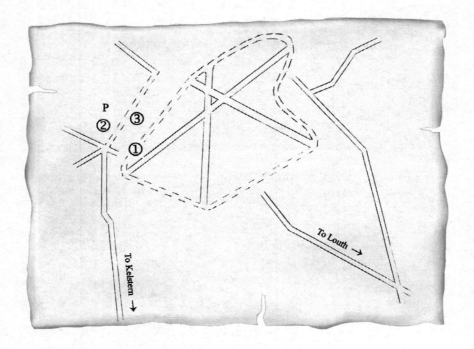

AT WAR

RAF Bomber Command Group 1. Operational 1943-45. A satellite of nearby RAF Binbrook, the base was home to the Lancasters of newly-formed 625 Squadron. During its existence, Kelstern despatched Lancasters for participation in most of the heavy bombing raids on German cities: Schweinfurt, Augsburg, Stuttgart, Frankfurt, Berlin, Essen and Nuremberg. 625 Squadron also participated in 'Operation

Manna'. Spread over eight days in April and May 1945, this mission comprised a series of food drops over the Netherlands. Following a hard winter, the Dutch were starving, and 11,000 tons of supplies were successfully delivered. Soon afterwards, 625 Squadron was transferred to RAF Scampton, bringing Kelstern's war to a close.

IN PEACE

Officially closed in October 1945, the land eventually reverting to agriculture. Fragments of the runways remain, with a few scattered wartime structures converted to farming use.

FEATURES OF INTEREST

Airfield Memorial (1).
Operations Block (2).
Squadron Roll of Honour, St Faith's Church, Kelstern.

The remaining stretch of the North Runway at Kelstern.

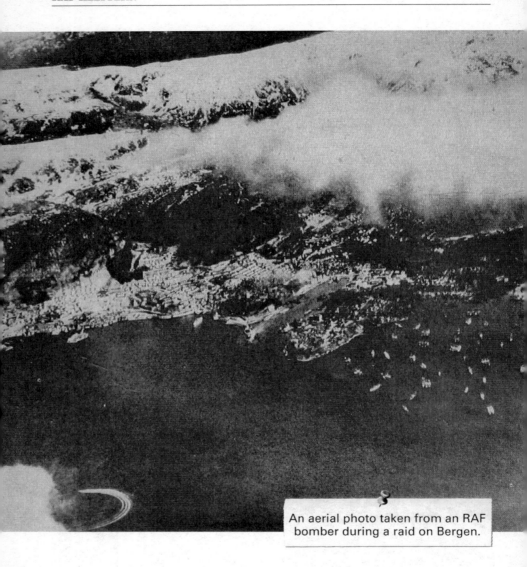

An aerial photo taken from an RAF bomber during a raid on Bergen.

EXPLORATION
The main airfield site is on private land and off-road walking is limited. Best viewed as an 'add on' to an RAF Binbrook visit.

TRIVIA
The Lancaster bomber's successor, the Lincoln, had a wingspan of 120 feet and could not be manoeuvred into a standard T2 hangar. Staff at RAF Kelstern devised a novel solution to the problem by setting tramlines in the concrete leading to a T2 hangar on the Technical Site, and then wheeling the Lincoln in sideways on a trolley. The hangar has gone, but the tramlines are still there (3).

CHECK OUT
625 Squadron RAF Memorial Association website.

The monument to No.625 Squadron at Kelstern that features a cut out of a Lancaster.

23. RAF Kirmington

Location: The airfield, the present-day Humberside Airport, is off the A18, 11 miles to the east of Grimsby.
Car Parking: On-road parking opposite St. Helen's Church, Kirmington (P).
Map: OS Explorer 281 (0910) & 284 (1011).
Refreshment: Marrowbone & Cleaver, Kirmington.

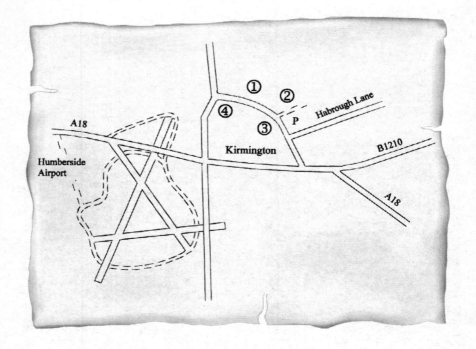

AT WAR

No 1 Group, Bomber Command. Operational 1942-45. Tasks of resident squadron 166 included mine-laying missions off the Frisian Islands. This work necessitated low-flying, so that if aircraft got into trouble, it was not always possible to bale out. When 166 Squadron's

A Vickers Wellington in pre-war, peacetime markings.

Wellington HF596 was attacked by enemy night-fighter ace, Hans Grimm, on 15/16 August 1943, it crashed into the North Sea. All five crew, of whom the eldest was 23, were killed. Sometimes, downed aircrew were picked up by resistance groups. On 3 August, Lancaster ME839 was flying over northern France when it was hit by a bomb released by another Lancaster flying above it. The flight engineer, Sergeant Sidney Witham, was smuggled into Spain by the French Resistance but by the time he made it home, the war had ended.

IN PEACE

At the end of the war, Kirmington was placed on Care & Maintenance until the mid-1950s when the land was returned to a agriculture. During the 1960s, a number of small airlines re-introduced flying on what remained of the main airfield site. Then it was decided that Kirmington was ideally placed for development as a regional airport. Finally, in March 1974, Humberside Airport opened for business.

A bomber crew returns to base after a mission. There would be little rest as debriefing and report-writing inevitably followed.

FEATURES OF INTEREST

166 Squadron Memorial & Memorial Garden (1).

WAAF Site (2).

Stained glass window memorial to 166 Squadron & Squadron Roll of Honour in St. Helen's Church (3).

Wartime photographs in Marrowbone & Cleaver (4).

Station bell and 166 Squadron Plaque in Airport terminal building.

EXPLORATION

Little remains of the original airfield, but a walk through Kirmington village is rewarding. The domestic sites were mainly situated in woodland to the north-east of the village, beyond Habrough Lane, where some good examples of red-brick blast shelters can be seen.

TRIVIA

The celebrated actor, Donald Pleasence served with 166 Squadron at RAF Kirmington. His Lancaster was shot down over Agenville on 31 August 1944 and he was taken prisoner. One of his best-known films is 'The Great Escape' in which, appropriately, he plays an RAF Officer who is a prisoner of war.

CHECK OUT

RAF 166 Squadron website.

St Helen's Church in Kirmington village has this memorial as well as a striking stained glass window commemorating the squadrons who flew from the airfield.

24. RAF Kirton in Lindsey

Location: On the B1398, off the A15, 16 miles to the north of Lincoln.
Car Parking: Layby parking on both sides of the road by Holt's Spar on the corner of High Street, Kirton-in-Lindsey (P).
Map: OS Explorer 281 (9794).
Refreshments: Queens Head, King Edward Street, Kirton in Lindsey.

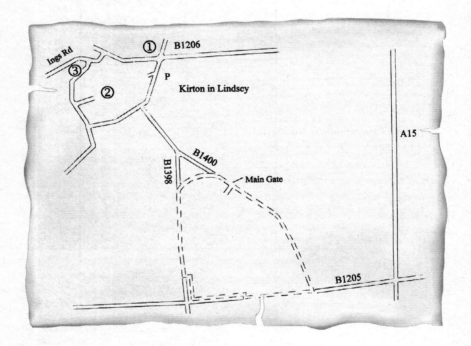

AT WAR

12 Group Fighter Command. Operational 1940-45. This pre-war expansion programme airfield was home to many squadrons. Lincolnshire was considered to be a quiet sector and fighter squadrons from the south-east were sent here to recuperate. The station was also used as a training ground for new squadrons. Pilots included Australians, New Zealanders, Poles and Americans. The latter formed

the 'Eagle' Squadrons   made up of volunteers who joined the RAF prior to American entering the war. There were three such squadrons: 71, 121 and 133. All spent time at Kirton in Lindsey.

IN PEACE

The station continued in a training role after the war. In 1966, it was handed over to the army, becoming 'Rapier Barracks'. A further period with the RAF followed from 2004, when it was used as an air control centre. The airfield has been put up for sale, although the Trent Valley Gliding Club, which uses a portion of the site, should remain in residence.

A squadron of Boulton Paul Defiants at Kirton in Lindsey. The Defiant was intended to be a bomber-killer, but never really succeeded in this role and was withdrawn from frontline service in 1941.

FEATURES OF INTEREST
Eagle Squadron memorial (to rear of war memorial on village green) (1).
133 Squadron plaque in St Andrew's Church (2).
Eagle Squadron graves (Ings Road cemetery) (3).

EXPLORATION
Difficult, given the uncertainty surrounding the future of the base. At time of writing, the site is boarded up and secured. A little of the interior can be seen from the B1398 and the main gate on the B1400.

TRIVIA
Towards the end of the war, Station Commander at Kirton in Lindsey was Group Captain John Hawtrey, a cousin of Charles Hawtrey, of 'Carry On' films fame. The Group Captain was as eccentric as his famous relative, once insisting that pilots in training should learn to skate.

WAAFs (Women's Auxillery Air Force) personnel on duty in a squadron operations room. The WAAFs provided essential administrative support.

A Hampden bomber being loaded with a marine mine. The Hampden bomb bay was specially designed to be able to take such large, bulky loads.

CHECK OUT

Trent Valley Gliding Club website for details of events/open days. Scunthorpe Telegraph website for information regarding the current status of the airfield.

The memorial at Kirton in Lindsey.

25. RAF Ludford Magna

Location: Off the A631 to the south of Ludford, 8½ miles west of Louth.
Car Parking: Village Hall car park (signposted off main road) in Ludford (P).
Map: OS Explorer 282 (2087).
Refreshments: White Hart Inn.

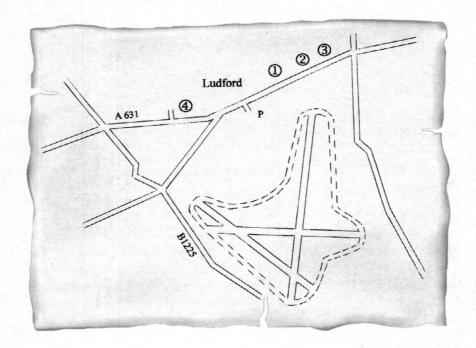

AT WAR

Group 1 Bomber Command. Operational 1943-45. Home to 101 Squadron. Missions included the Nuremberg Raid (30/31 March 1944), when seven of 101 Squadron's Lancasters were lost. The Squadron's main claim to fame lay in its use of detection equipment to counter the threat from enemy night fighters in particular, the system known as 'Airborne Cigar'. Essentially, this involved the installation of a special radio and the addition of an eighth, German-speaking member of the air crew to operate it. The operator could seek out radio frequencies used by the night fighters and then jam the broadcasts. Ludford Magna was closed to flying in October 1945, by which time 101 Squadron had taken part in more raids than any other squadron of Group 1 Bomber Command and had suffered the highest wartime casualty rate of any RAF squadron.

IN PEACE

After the war, Ludford Magna's domestic sites were used to accommodate ex-servicemen as well as many Polish refugees, who were still arriving as late as 1948. Between 1959 and 1963, the station took on a new lease of life as a Thor Missile Base. Today, the main airfield site is farmland. The airfield perimeter track is well-preserved and the location of the three missile launch pads is discernible.

FEATURES OF INTEREST

Airfield Memorial (1).
101 Squadron Roll of Honour in Church of St Mary & St Peter (2).
101 Squadron Memorial plaque on wall of White Hart Inn (3).
Well preserved domestic site at 'Brooklyn' along the 'Permissive Footpath' beyond Sixhills Lane (4).

A Lancaster parked on the ground at Ludford Magna. A total of 7,377 Lancasters were built, but only two remain airworthy.

A photograph of the centre of Bremen taken from a Lancaster a few days after Germany surrendered in 1945. The awesome destructive power wielded by Bomber Command is clear.

EXPLORATION

The domestic sites were situated to the north of the village. A fragmented public footpath system facilitates partial exploration. In addition to the surviving structures at Brooklyn, more can be seen in a small garden centre complex, fronted by the Viking Way Coffee House.

TRIVIA

Aircrew often had wry pet names for their airfields. Goxhill was 'Goat Hill', and Sandtoft was 'Prangtoft'. Owing to its poor drainage, Ludford Magna soon became 'Mudford Magna'.

Wartime Nissen Huts still standing at Ludford Magna.

TO SERVE WAS THEIR HIGHEST AIM

CHECK OUT
Polish Resettlement Camps in the UK 1946 website.

The monument erected beside the main village street in 1978 Ludford Magna.

26. RAF Metheringham

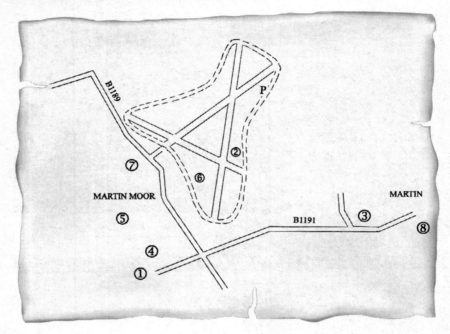

Location: On the B1189, 2 miles to the east of Metheringham.
Car Parking: Designated parking area on the minor road to Blankney Fen (P) and/or Airfield Visitor Centre.
Map: OS Explorer 273 (6010).
Refreshments: Royal Oak, Martin (8).

AT WAR

5 Group Bomber Command. Operational 1943-46. Home to 106 Squadron. Participated in many significant missions, including the Battle of Berlin and raids on the V1 flying-bomb storage sites. Metheringham was one of only five Lincolnshire bases (along with Fiskerton, Ludford Magna, Manston and Sturgate) to be equipped with FIDO (Fog Investigation and Dispersal Operation), designed to help pilots land in the fog which often enveloped the Fens. A series of

fuel burners lining the main runway and burning petrol at the rate of 100,000 gallons per hour, would produce sufficient heat to lift the fog and render the runway visible.

IN PEACE

Flying ceased in the spring of 1946 and Metheringham was placed on Care & Maintenance. The site was eventually sold in 1961. Current usage is a mix of agriculture and light industry. A visitor centre has been fashioned from the only remaining Domestic Site (No. 4).

The museum at RAF Metheringham, which is open at weekends through the summer.

The mess staff of the Airmen's Canteen, photographed in about 1943.

FEATURES OF INTEREST

Airfield Visitor Centre (1). Includes memorial garden and restored buildings.

106 Squadron Airfield Memorial (2)

106 Squadron Memorial Plaque in Holy Trinity Church, Martin (3). Open late morning after services on first and third Sundays of the month.

Airfield Water Tower (4)

Sick Quarters Site (5)

Control Tower (6). Probably being converted into a private residence.

Guard Room (7), developed into Eclipse Farm Shop.

EXPLORATION

Good access to the main airfield site. The perimeter track survives, and the existing minor road to Blankney formed the nucleus of a secondary runway. Excellent walking.

TRIVIA

It remains unclear as to how names for airfields were chosen. RAF Metheringham is adjacent to the village of Martin, so 'RAF Martin' would appear to be more logical. Apparently, the nearest settlement which had a railway station was a significant factor in reaching a decision. This would work in the present case, although there are many examples that defy explanation.

The imposing memorial on the site of RAF Metheringham. A phantom young lady reportedly haunts the area.

CHECK OUT

Metheringham Airfield Visitor Centre website.
British Pathé website for a 1946 RAF Film Unit production about FIDO, with creaky footage of RAF Metheringham. (Additional Pathé offerings include footage of racing driver, Raymond Mays, at Folkingham in 1949).

27. RAF North Coates

Location: Off the A1031 7 miles to the south of Grimsby.
Car Parking: North Coates Flying Club (P).
Map: OS Explorer 283 (3602).
Refreshments: Flying Club café or The Crown & Anchor, Tetney Lock.

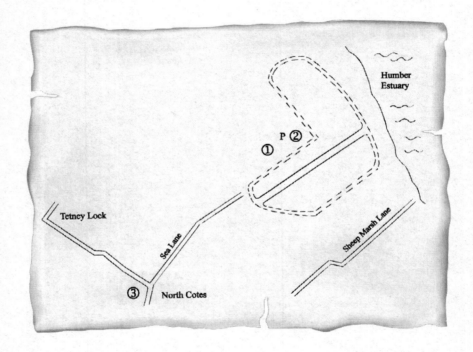

AT WAR

16 Group Coastal Command. Operational 1939-45. The station was functional during the 1930s, but was considered too close to the east coast for comfort at the outbreak of war and it was the spring of 1940 before squadrons of Bristol Blenheims and Beauforts moved in to carry out raids on enemy shipping conveys. The famous North Coates Strike Wing, comprising three squadrons (143, 236 and 254) was formed in the autumn of 1942. The strategy was for two conventionally armed

110

squadrons to pave the way for the third, equipped with torpedoes (and, later, rockets) to strike targets within convoys. Results were mixed and although there were successes, casualties were relatively high.

IN PEACE

After the war, North Coates took on a bomb disposal role. For a time, it served as a helicopter air-sea rescue base. Throughout the 1960s, and again in the 1980s, the station accommodated Bloodhound missiles. In the early 1990s, the site was sold off. It now comprises private housing, developed from the RAF accommodation blocks and acts as a centre for a missionary society (New Tribes mission). The future of North Coates Flying Club, also based here, is currently (2014) threatened by offshore wind farm development.

The entrance to the North Coates Flying Club, which now occupies the airfield.

The wreckage of a Lancaster of No.576 Squadron that crased on take off in 1944.

FEATURES OF INTEREST

North Coates Strike wing Memorial (1).
Heritage Collection (small museum operated by Flying Club) (2).
St. Nicholas Church, North Cotes (stained glass window/Roll of Honour/RAF graves in churchyard) (3).

EXPLORATION

There is easy access to the site, although many structures have disappeared. Enter by the main gate and drive up Kenneth Campbell Road. The Flying Club is at the top. An imposing Strike Squadron memorial, with statue, is located on the sea front at Cleethorpes. A miniature version of the statue, mounted on a plinth, has been removed from North Coates, although the inscribed plinth remains, situated on the left hand side of Kenneth Campbell Road on the approach to the Flying Club.

TRIVIA

Budding entertainer, Max Bygraves, served as a member of the ground crew at RAF North Coates, during which time he staged a revue appropriately entitled 'Chocks Away'.

CHECK OUT

North Coates Flying Club website for details of events/open days.

A reconnaisance photo of the German warship Scharnhorst in Kiel. Although the RAF attempted to bomb the warship several times, she was eventually sunk by the Royal Navy during the Battle of North Cape on 26 December 1943.

28. RAF North Killingholme

Location: On East Halton Road, off the A160, 2 miles to the north-west of Immingham.
Car Parking: Church Lane, North Killingholme (P).
Map: OS Explorer 284 (1317).
Refreshments: Ashbourne Hotel, North Killingholme.

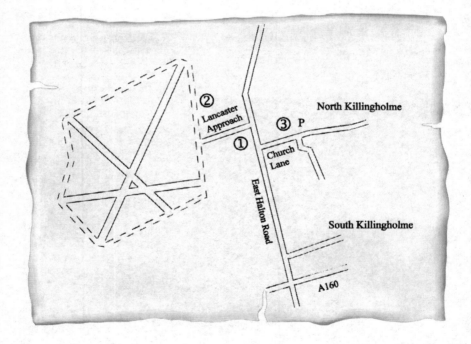

AT WAR

Group 1 Bomber Command. Operational 1943-45. A late starter, North Killingholme had to wait until the beginning of 1944 before receiving a squadron   550, from Grimsby. Even so, 550 Squadron went on to complete nearly 200 missions, sustaining relatively low losses (1.6%) in the process. Lancaster LL811 ('Bad Penny II') of 550

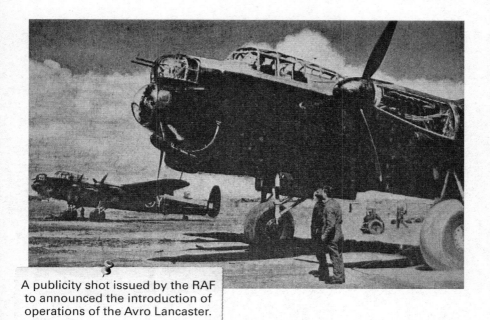

A publicity shot issued by the RAF to announced the introduction of operations of the Avro Lancaster.

Squadron is credited with dropping the first bombs of the D-Day campaign.

IN PEACE
The station was closed to flying soon after the war ended and the land eventually sold off. The main airfield site is given over to a mix of agriculture and light industry, operating against a backdrop of oil refineries.

FEATURES OF INTEREST
Squadron memorial and Information Panel (on Lancaster Approach) (1).
B1 hangar (2).
Stained glass window and plaque in St. Denys' Church (3).
550 Squadron museum (Village Hall).

The village sign for North Killingholme commemorates its RAF heritage.

EXPLORATION

Church and village hall stand side by side and there is a little roadside parking in addition to the village hall car park. Note the memorial bench and the evocative village sign. The memorial is perched precariously on the corner of Lancaster Approach. Visitors need to park further along the road or, perhaps, walk up from the village. Some buildings on the main airfield site and the domestic sites (situated between East Halton Road and the oil refineries) survive on private land. However, a track at the end of Lancaster Approach, by the Volvo Construction Equipment site, yields a B1 hangar (in middle distance) and a few crumbling maycrete buildings. The base's watering-hole, The Cross Keys, has been closed and boarded-up for some time.

TRIVIA

The need for new airfields helped to drag Britain's construction industry into the twentieth century. The construction companies notably Laing, McAlpine and Wimpey (which won the contract for North Killingholme)   laid the runways with the help of heavy plant shipped over from America as part of the lend-lease programme.

CHECK OUT

550 Squadron & North Killingholme Association superb website for background information, details of special events and access to museum and church. (Information Panel also notes village hall keyholders, and the church information board gives keyholder data).

The monument at North Killingholme. There parish church of St Denys boasts a fine stained glass window dedicated to those who served at the airbase.

29. RAF/USAAF North Witham

Location: On the A151, ½ mile west of the A1/Colsterworth junction.
Car Parking: Entrance to Twyford Wood. (P)
Map: OS Explorer 247 (9422).
Refreshments: Colsterworth Services/White Lion, Colsterworth.

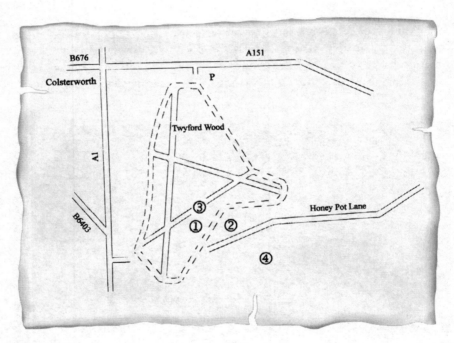

AT WAR

Operational 1943-1945. The site was originally chosen as an airfield for Bomber Command. By the time it was ready to open, towards the end of 1943, the Americans were hungry for space, and it was handed over to the American 9th Army Air Force. From December 1943, North Witham functioned largely as a maintenance unit, preparing new Douglas C-47 transport aircraft for delivery to operational airfields. However, in March 1944, the 9th Troop Carrier Command Pathfinder Group School arrived to prepare for the D-Day landings.

Bomber crews celebrate after returning from a successful raid.

Small 'Pathfinder groups of parachutists were trained to precede the Airborne Divisions and place radar beacons near the drop zones. When the big day came, North Witham was the first USAAF base to get men in the air for Operation Overlord, 20 C-47s taking off for Normandy. In May 1945, the base was handed back to the RAF and used for bomb storage.

IN PEACE

The airfield was eventually closed in 1956 and taken over by the Forestry Commission for redevelopment as woodland. For a time, British Motor Racing used the runways as a testing ground, and motor rallies still occasionally take place. The woods are a sanctuary for rare butterflies and the site is occasionally used as a location by film studios. The three runways are largely intact, as is nearly all of the encircling perimeter track.

FEATURES OF INTEREST
Control Tower (Type 12779/41) (1). Currently threatened with demolition.
Refurbished T2 hangar (2).
Bomb-loading ramp (3).
Water Tower (4).

EXPLORATION
North Witham is one of the few remaining old airfield sites where the visitor can roam at will. A public footpath runs through the extreme southern portion of the site, with a gate (which should be unlocked) permitting access to Honeypot Lane.

TRIVIA
On the afternoon of 24 September 1944, Glenn Miller and the American Band of the AEF gave a morale-boosting 60 minute concert to 2,500 airborne troops crammed into one of North Witham's two 'T2' hangars.

The old control tower at North Witham, now surrounded by saplings planted by the Forestry Commission.

CHECK OUT
Twyford Wood (England)   Forestry Commission website.

A pair of photos issued by the RAF after a raid on Mainz to show the destruction wrought. The city before the raid is in the top photo, while the same area after is shown below.

30. RAF Sandtoft

Location: Between Westgate and Sandtoft, 7 miles to the west of Scunthorpe. Exit M180 at Junction 2. Take the A161 southbound (signposted to Epworth). The Westgate/Sandtoft road is off to the right, after about a mile.
Car Parking: Sandtoft Flying Club (P) or by the River Torne.
Map: OS Explorer 280 (7507).
Refreshments: Sandtoft Flying Club/The Reindeer Inn, Thorne Road, Sandtoft.

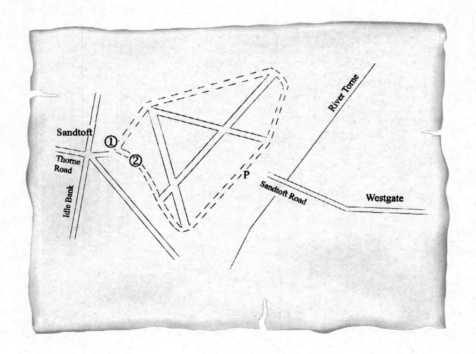

AT WAR

Group 1 Bomber Command station, operational 1943-45. Home to Heavy Conversion Unit 1667 from February 1944. HCUs were designed to help crews experienced in operating medium bombers to

An unusual photo of a formation of Lancasters flying in daylight hours.

transfer to four-engine heavy bombers which, by 1944, usually meant Lancasters. However, aircrews arriving at Sandtoft discovered that they would be training on battle-weary Handley Page Halifaxes, most of which were unfit for service. Officially, they were described as 'operationally tired'. To the air crews who flew in them, they were simply 'clapped out' and even the toughest of pilots would occasionally refuse to take them up. Thus, the history of RAF Sandtoft is a sad catalogue of accidents which occurred in the skies over the airfield and surrounding villages. Towards the end of 1944, Lancasters began arriving as replacements for the Halifaxes, and HCU 1667 continued to operate until November 1945.

IN PEACE

In 1953, Sandtoft was identified for development as a reserve USAAF base but nothing came of it, and towards the end of the decade, the land was sold. Much of the main airfield site is given over to light industrial use   the layout following the course of the runways. The Trolleybus Museum was established on the Technical Site in 1969 and the Sandtoft Flying Club, utilising a portion of the eastern perimeter track, reintroduced flying in 1982.

The main plotting room at Bomber Command HQ.

FEATURES OF INTEREST
Airfield Memorial (1) (in private grounds).
Control Tower (2) (private residence).

EXPLORATION

Sandtoft Road (closed during the war years) runs through the centre of the main airfield site. A Sunday visit cuts out the HGV traffic. The Control Tower a white building flanked by a couple of wartime structures, is located opposite Powell Engineering. The Airfield Memorial, visible from the road, occupies the site of the airfield's radio station look for the green barrier.

TRIVIA

The war created a severe housing shortage. With the closure of airfields, many control towers were converted into houses, in which guise several have survived to the present day.

CHECK OUT

The Wartime Memories Project RAF Sandtoft website.
Sandtoft Squatters Camp website.

The memorial at Sandtoft is surrounded by a small garden and stands on one of the old living sites.

31. RAF Scampton

Location: On the A15, miles to the north of Lincoln. Scampton village is on the western edge of the airfield, on the B1398.
Car Parking: Use Viewpoint (P) at corner of B1398 and A1500 and walk into the village.
Map: OS Explorer 272 (9679).
Refreshments: Dambusters Inn.

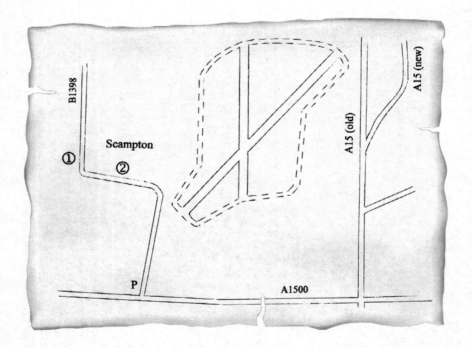

AT WAR

1 Group, Bomber Command. Operational 1939-45. An ex-First World War Airfield, Scampton was re-developed during the 1930s. By September 1939, 49 and 83 Squadrons were in residence 49 Squadron being the first RAF squadron to fly the Handley Page Hampden. Three Victoria Crosses were awarded to aircrew flying from the station: to

Flight-Lieutenant R Learoyd of 49 Squadron; Sergeant John Hannah of 83 Squadron and, most famously, to Wing Commander Guy Gibson of 617 Squadron. Gibson led the mission to breach the Ruhr dams 'Operation Chastise', as it was called. The assault, which took place on 16/17 May 1943, succeeded in breaching the Mohne and Eder Dams, but at a heavy cost: eight of the nineteen Lancasters involved failed to return.

IN PEACE

Scampton accommodated American B-29s during the Berlin Airlift in 1948-49, and went on to house English Electric Canberras and Avro Vulcans. The arrival of the latter led to a lengthening of the main runway and a consequent diversion of the A15. In 1996, the station closed but, thankfully, re-opened in 2000 to provide a home for the Red Arrows display team.

A Handley Page Hampden bomber wearing pre-war peacetime markings. These were quickly replaced with coded markings after war broke out.

A sentry stands outside the entrance to a command bunker.

FEATURES OF INTEREST

RAF Scampton Heritage Centre (within base).
Memorial to Guy Gibson's Labrador (within base).
4 C Type hangars.
RAF Chapel and squadron memorial plaques in Church of St. John the Baptist/War Graves & The John Hannah Rose Garden in churchyard (1).
The Dambusters Inn (contains memorabilia) (2).

EXPLORATION

There are a couple of public tracks   one leading from Aisthorpe to the western perimeter of the airfield and another, constituting the old course of the A15, used by plane spotters. It is best to use the Viewpoint for parking and walk up into the village.

TRIVIA
'Just Jane', (Lancaster NX 611) housed at East Kirkby's Lincolnshire Aviation Heritage Centre spent 10 years (1973-83) as 'gate guardian' at RAF Scampton. Between 1960 and 1970, gate guardian was Lancaster R5868, the oldest surviving Lancaster (born 1942), now at the RAF Museum, Hendon.

CHECK OUT
RAF Scampton Station Home Page website for visiting arrangements.

A wall at RAF Scampton featuring shields bearing the badges of squadrons that have served here.

32. RAF Skellingthorpe

Location: On the B1190, 3 miles to the south-west of Lincoln city centre.
Car Parking: Birchwood Community & Leisure Centre (P) /Skellingthorpe Community Centre.
Map: OS Explorer 272 (6993).
Refreshments: The Black Swan, Jasmin Road, Birchwood.

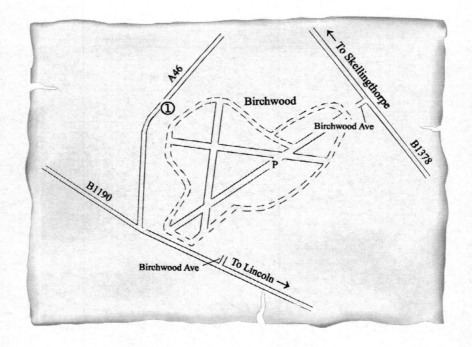

AT WAR

5 Group Bomber Command. Operational 1941-45. The first unit in residence was 50 Squadron. For displaying 'determination and valour of the highest order' during a raid on Cologne on 30/31 May 1942, Flying Officer Leslie Manser of 50 Squadron was posthumously awarded the Victoria Cross. In November 1943, 61 Squadron arrived.

Pilot Officer Leslie Manser who was awarded a posthumous Victoria Cross after saving his crew at the cost of his own life during a raid on Cologne in 1942.

One of its pilots, Flight Lieutenant Bill Reid, had just been awarded the Victoria Cross for his actions during a raid on Dusseldorf on 3/4 November 1943. Apart from a few short weeks, 50 & 61 Squadrons operated together from Skellingthorpe for the rest of the war.

IN PEACE

The station continued to be used by the RAF largely for storage until the early 1950s. At one stage, there were tentative proposals for the development of a civil airport here, but these came to nothing. From the late 1960s, housing began to encroach on the site. Development continued apace throughout the 1970s until the airfield was obliterated.

FEATURES OF INTEREST

61 Squadron Memorial & Museum (Birchwood Community & Leisure Centre, Birchwood Avenue, Birchwood).
Airfield Memorial & photographic exhibition on Heritage Room, Skellingthorpe Community Centre, Lincoln Road, Skellingthorpe.

EXPLORATION

Given the fact that the main airfield site is buried beneath the Birchwood housing development, exploration is largely academic, although remains of the bomb storage site can be seen, marked as Skellingthorpe Moor Plantation on OS Explorer 272 (9270) (1). Do not confuse the Birchwood Community & Leisure Centre with the Birchwood (shopping) Centre which is a little further south on Birchwood Avenue, the main road running through the development.

The city centre of Cologne showing the damage inflicted by RAF Bomber Command. Despite appearances, the cathedral was hit several times but survived.

The Leslie Manser School, built on part of the old Skellingthorpe air base.

TRIVIA

Bomber aircrews were notoriously superstitious. Sometimes, an aircraft was thought to be unlucky, and might even be deliberately ditched as a result. At other times, it was noticed that men who dated a particular WAAF failed to return from operations, and the unfortunate girl would be treated as a pariah. 50 Squadron's pet superstition lay in the necessity of listening to a recording of the Andrews Sisters singing 'The Shrine of St. Cecilia' prior to setting out on a mission.

CHECK OUT

No. 50 and No. 61 Squadrons Association website.

The war memorial at Skellingthorpe, which is engraved with images of Hampden, Manchester and Lancaster bombers.

33. RAF Spilsby

Location: 3 miles to the east of Spilsby, off a minor road (closed during the war) which branches off the B1195 between the villages of Halton Holegate and Great Steeping.
Car Parking: Airfield Memorial (P).
Map: OS Explorer 274 (4465).
Refreshments: The Bell, Halton Holegate.

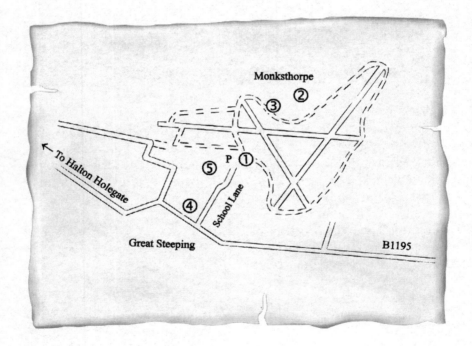

AT WAR

Group 5 Bomber Command. Operational October 1943-November 1946. The first occupants were the crews of 207 Squadron, flying Lancasters. The squadron played a full role in the bombing campaign against Berlin in the winter of 1943/44. Later missions included a raid on the synthetic oil plants at Wesseling and Schloven/Buer on the evening of 21/22 June 1944 - during which five of Spilsby's Lancasters fell victim to enemy night-fighters - and sorties in support of the D-Day landings. In September 1944, 44 Squadron arrived from RAF Dunholme Lodge to work in tandem with 207 Squadron until the end of the war. In October 1945, Spilsby was selected as the site for an Armament Practice School, which functioned until November 1946.

IN PEACE

In 1955, the airfield was re-opened as a non-operational USAF base. Three years later, it closed for good, the land reverting to agricultural use. The runways have long-since vanished, but a portion of the perimeter track and a few hardstandings remain.

A Lancaster drops a 4,000lb "cookie" bomb plus a mass of incendiaries during a raid on Duisberg in 1945.

The surviving T2 hangar at Spilsby. The T2 was a lightweight structure intended to last only a few years, so such survivors are rare.

FEATURES OF INTEREST

New Airfield Memorial (1).
Old Airfield Memorial (2).
B1 hangar (3).
207 & 44 Squadron Memorials, Church of All Saints, Great Steeping (4).
Remains of Operations Block (5).
The Bell, Halton Holegate (dedicated to 207 & 44 Squadrons).

EXPLORATION

Minor roads straddle the main airfield site, facilitating exploration. A new memorial was put in place in 2012, and its predecessor removed to the Monksthorpe Baptist Chapel (accessible via the track which crosses the airfield, via the B1 Hangar.) The remains of the Operations Block are almost across the road from the new Memorial.

TRIVIA
Initially, the Air Ministry intended to use the house and grounds of adjacent Gunby Hall in the construction of the airfield. The Hall's owners (the Massingberd family) successfully appealed directly to King George VI, resulting in the site being shifted to the south-west.

CHECK OUT
207 Squadron Association website.
National Trust Website re: Gunby Hall & Monksthorpe Baptist Chapel.

The memorial at Spilsby, which was erected in 2001.

34. RAF Strubby

Location: At Woodthorpe, on the B1373, 4 miles to the north of Alford. Follow the 'Lincs Aquatics' sign.
Car Parking: Main Airfield site (P) or adjacent Garden Centre.
Map: OS Explorer 274 (4480).
Refreshments: Garden Centre restaurant (décor includes photographs of wartime airfield).

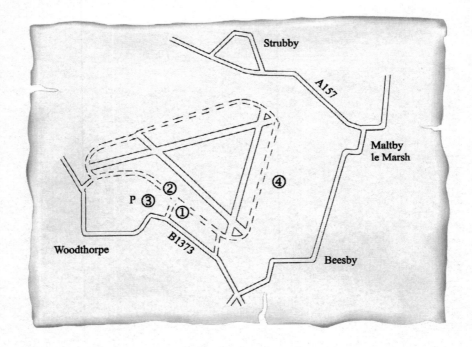

AT WAR

Operational 1944-45. Initially (May 1944) Group 16, RAF Coastal Command, with 280 Squadron, flying the Vickers Warwick ASR1 a bomber converted into an air-sea rescue vehicle. (A lifeboat was attached to the undercarriage and could be dropped into the sea.) Next to arrive were Squadrons 141 and 404, with Bristol Beaufighters to

The derelict, but largely intact, control tower at RAF Strubby.

make air strikes on enemy merchant shipping. In September 1944, Strubby was transferred to Group 5 Bomber Command, with 619 Squadron arriving from RAF Dunholme Lodge. Among 619's many missions was a devastating attack on railway marshalling yards at Heilbronn on the night of 4/5 December 1944. The yards were destroyed, but incendiary bombs started a firestorm, decimating much of the city and killing over 6,500 people. Strubby was closed to flying in September 1945 and the site used for storage.

IN PEACE

Between 1949 and 1972, Strubby resumed flying operations as a RLG for RAF Manby. For twenty years, from the mid-1970s, ConocoPhillips used the north-east portion of the site as a heliport to service its north-sea oil rigs. Current activities include gliding with the Lincolnshire Gliding Club, go-karting and model aircraft flying.

Old buildings still standing at the site of RAF Strubby.

FEATURES OF INTEREST
Airfield Memorial (1).
Control Tower (2) (private residence).
T2 hangar (3) (reconditioned, housing Lincs Aquatics).
B2 hangar (4).
Many preserved maycrete structures

EXPLORATION
A public footpath, utilising the eastern portion of the perimeter track, runs across the airfield, skirting the B2 Hangar.

TRIVIA
Unfortunately, old airfields make good building plots, for everything from prisons to housing estates. Over the years, Strubby has fought off its share of developers   most recently central government, which proposed using it as a site for a 5,000 home 'eco-town'.

CHECK OUT
Woodthorpe Caravan and Leisure Park website.

A Beaufighter operating out of RAF Strubby. This versatile aircraft entered service in 1940 as a nightfighter, but later saw service as a torpedo bomber and ground attack aircraft.

The "old" memorial at RAF Strubby is in fact a memorial to Flt Lt Peter Le Brocq. The "new" memorial commemorates the base as a whole.

35. RAF Sutton Bridge

Location: The airfield lies to the south-east of Sutton Bridge, off the A17, 10 miles to the east of Kings Lynn.
Car Parking: On-road parking (P) by the church on Bridge Road, the main road running through the village.
Map: OS Explorer 249 (4820).
Refreshments: Riverside Bar & Restaurant, Bridge Road.

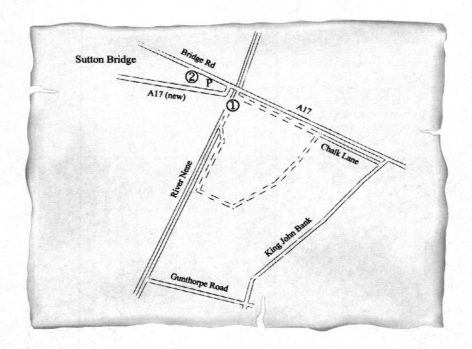

AT WAR

RAF Sutton Bridge began life in 1926 as one of the RAF's Summer Armament Practice Camps. Three operational squadrons were temporarily based here in late 1939, but Sutton Bridge's finest hour was the period March 1940-March 1942 when, as 6   and then 56 Operational Training Unit, it served as a base for training Hawker

Hurricane pilots. The Germans were aware of the vital importance of this work. On the evening of 10/11 May 1941, for example, the station was hit by no less than three enemy raids which destroyed/damaged several Hurricanes.

In March 1942, Sutton Bridge again changed roles, becoming the Central Gunnery School, training fighter pilots and bomber crews in air gunnery skills. In charge of fighter pilot training was Adolph 'Sailor' Malan, celebrated South African 'Ace', credited with 27 enemy kills. Indeed, Sutton Bridge was a truly cosmopolitan base, accommodating Americans, Poles, French, Czechs and many other nationalities. The CGS moved to RAF Catfoss in April 1944, Sutton Bridge ending its flying days as a satellite of RAF Peterborough.

A squadron operations room photographed in 1940. Note the model aircraft hanging from the ceiling, used for identification tests.

A debriefing session photographed in 1940. The air crew are describing their raid to the intelligence officer.

IN PEACE

Flying ceased at Sutton Bridge in April 1946. For the next twelve years, the base was used for storage, after which the land reverted to agriculture, although light industry now predominates.

FEATURES OF INTEREST

Airfield Memorial (1).

Chapel of St. Michael (in St. Matthew's Church), dedicated to Commonwealth servicemen who lost their lives while stationed at RAF Sutton Bridge. RAF war graves section in churchyard (2).

EXPLORATION
Little to see on the main airfield site, with the skyline dominated by a power station, but a circular walk is possible, via the minor road system, with an occasional foray onto the airfield itself, courtesy of the industrial estate's access roads.

TRIVIA
Grass airfields   of which there were many   often degenerated into a sea of mud during the winter months. Sutton Bridge benefited from having part of its surface underpinned with steel matting.

CHECK OUT
Bridge Watch Sutton Bridge website.

The chapel in St Matthew's Church, Sutton Bridge, that is dedicated to the RAF.

36. RAF Swinderby

Location: Witham St. Hughs, off the A46, 8 miles to the south-west of Lincoln.
Car Parking: Witham St. Hughs Village Hall (P) or adjacent Co-op car park.
Map: OS Explorer 271 (8861).
Refreshments: The Dovecote, Fosse Way (A46).

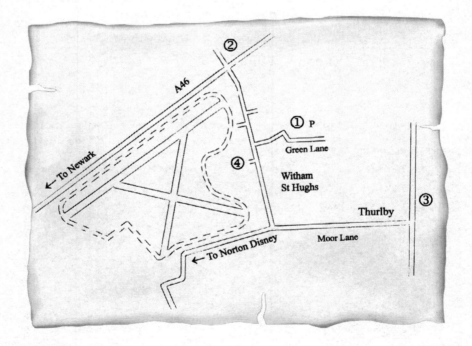

AT WAR

5 Group Bomber Command. Operational 1939-45. Swinderby was one of the last pre-war expansion airfields. The first arrivals were 300 and 301 (Polish) Squadrons with their Fairey Battles. From 1942, following the installation of concrete runways, Swinderby took on a training role with 1660 HCU. Lancasters were still in short supply,

A Lancaster operating out of Swinderby. The Lancaster was defended by eight machine guns mounted in three hydraulically powered turrets.

necessitating use of Halifaxes and Stirlings. There would be many accidents, inevitable in training, but the change of function meant that casualties sustained on the night of 23/24 September 1942 during a raid on Wismar represented Swinderby's last operational losses of the war.

IN PEACE

The station survived the airfield closure period immediately after the war, continuing in its training role   including a stint as RAF School of Recruit Training   until 1993. Today, the site is shared by a business park and the new community of Witham St. Hughs.

FEATURES OF INTEREST

Airfield memorial and Information Panel (outside Village Hall, Green Lane) (1).

The Dovecote (RAF Swinderby's watering-hole) contains some memorabilia (2).

RAF graves in St. Germain's churchyard, Thurlby (3).

300 & 301 Squadron memorial and plaque in St. Peter's Church, Norton Disney.

The Battle of Britain Memorial Flight Lancaster P474, which entered service in 1945 on reconnaissance duties.

EXPLORATION

The wartime buildings are gradually being whittled away, and exploration is now largely confined to short car journeys between memorials. Entering from the A46, two T2 hangars are visible at the first left turn. The main business park site is on the right and you can drive in to see two J Type hangars. The new village is to the left (Warren Lane) at the next roundabout. This leads on to Green Lane, which was the access road between the main airfield site and the domestic site. What used to be the main entrance to RAF Swinderby (4) is boarded up a sorry sight indeed.

TRIVIA

RAF bases were often the focus of morale-boosting visits by royalty. King George VI and Queen Elizabeth toured RAF Digby on 9 July 1940 and RAF North Coates on 27 May 1943. RAF Swinderby received its royal visit on 22 January 1941.

CHECK OUT

Witham St Hughs Parish Council Website.

The information board outside the new village hall that gives the history of the airfield.

37. RAF Waddington

Location: On the A607, 3 miles to the south of Lincoln.
Car Parking: Bar Lane, Waddington and Viewing Area (A15) (P).
Map: OS Explorer 272 (9864).
Refreshments: The Wheatsheaf, Waddington/ The Sentry Post in Viewing Area.

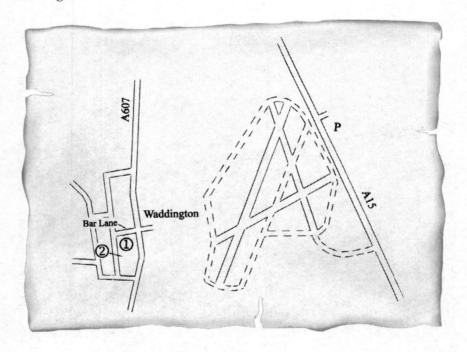

AT WAR

Bomber Command Group 5. Operational 1939-45. In fact, RAF Waddington began life in 1916 with the Royal Flying Corps and is still very much alive. As part of the 1930s expansion programme, the station was well placed to go into action on the day war was declared (3rd September 1939) when Hampdens of 44 Squadron were despatched to search for enemy shipping. Many squadrons served at

Waddington, but 44 (Rhodesia) Squadron, as it came to be known, stayed until 1943. It received the first Avro Lancasters off the production line and also went on to suffer the third heaviest losses in Bomber Command. By the end of the war, Waddington itself had lost the highest number of aircraft of any bomber airfield.

IN PEACE

Waddington's post-war activities include a period (1948-51) as a reserve United States Air Force base and, during the 1950s, operation of the English Electric Canberra followed by the Avro Vulcan, which played a significant role in the Falklands War. Today, Boeing Sentry and Raytheon Sentinel surveillance aircraft are based here, and Reaper UAVs (drones) are controlled from the station. During 2015, the main runway will be re-laid and extended.

Wireless operators under training. They are being fed morse code radio messages through their earphones while flying in a noise aircraft to simulate operational conditions.

FEATURES OF INTEREST
Airfield memorial (within the base).
Heritage Centre (within the base).
Clock memorial & plaque in Bar Lane (1).
Foundation stone of modern St. Michael's Church, Waddington (2)
(noting that the original church was destroyed in a bombing raid).
RAF graves in churchyard.

EXPLORATION
Obviously limited. A couple of truncated public footpaths lead to the
perimeter fence, but the best time to visit is during the Waddington
International Air Show. Information Boards in the Viewing Area.

TRIVIA
During its early days, Royal
Flying Corps Waddington's
trainees included Russian
'Whites' who were fighting the
Bolshevik 'Reds' in the Russian
Revolution.

CHECK OUT
Waddington International
Airshow website.
RAF Waddington Heritage
Centre website for information
about exhibits and admission.

The memorial at RAF Waddington
takes the form of this clock
mounted on a pole and dedicated
to the Australians who lost their
lives while serving here.

A pair of mechanics outside the radar building in about 1944. By this date radar was being used on a more localised basis than in the Battle of Britain.

38. RAF Wellingore

Location: Off Pottergate Road, running parallel with the A607, 2 miles to the south of Navenby.
Car Parking: Viewpoint, Pottergate Road (P).
Map: Ordnance Survey Explorer 272 (9854).
Refreshments: Lion & Royal, High Street, Navenby.

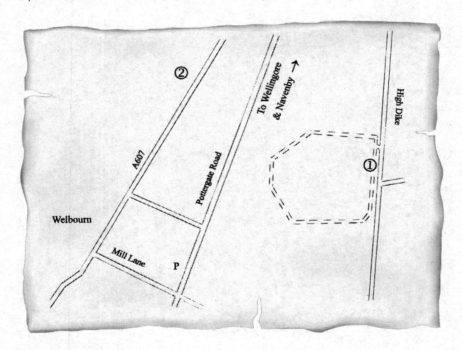

AT WAR

Fighter Command Group 12. Operational 1939-45. An ex-World War I airfield, Wellingore was used as a Relief Landing Ground for RAF Cranwell in the 1930s. In 1940, it became an RLG for RAF Digby. Early resident units included 29 Squadron with Bristol Blenheims and 412 (RCAF) Squadron. Flying with the latter was the Canadian war poet, John Magee, killed on 11 December 1941 in a collision with an

Airspeed Oxford on during a training flight. Among later visitors were 613 Squadron with Mustangs and 349 (Belgian) Squadron, flying Spitfires.

IN PEACE

After the war, the base continued to function for a time as a Prisoner of War camp for Germans and Ukranians, who worked on local farms. Flying continued until 1947, after which the site was returned to agricultural use.

The Lion and Royal pub, a favoured watering hole for officers from RAF Wellingore.

By the spring of 1945 the German air defence were so weak that for the first time since 1940 the RAF ventured to bomb targets by daylight.

FEATURES OF INTEREST:
Battle HQ (1).
Wellingore Hall (requisitioned for RAF use).
Lion & Royal, Navenby.

EXPLORATION
A public footpath, linking Pottergate Road and High Dike, crosses the north-east corner of the perimeter track which survives almost in its entirety. Paved footpaths and wide grass verges facilitate exploration of the area. Precious little remains of the domestic site (later used for housing POWs) on the western side of Pottergate Road (2). The Battle HQ is in the hedgerow on the western side of High Dike, between the Viking Way marker and the public footpath leading across the airfield. Wellingore Hall lies on Hall Street in Wellingore.

TRIVIA
In November 1941, Guy Gibson joined 29 Squadron. Newly married, he and his wife, Eve, lodged at the Lion & Royal. Gibson (who hated Lincolnshire) noted that the inn's main attraction was the presence of a bath.

CHECK OUT
Wikipaedia website entry for John Gillespie Magee Jr.

39. RAF Wickenby

Location: On the B 1399, off the A158, 11 miles to the north-east of Lincoln.
Car Parking: Wickenby Airfield (P).
Map: Ordnance Survey Explorer 282 (1081).
Refreshments: Wickenby Airfield Tea Room.

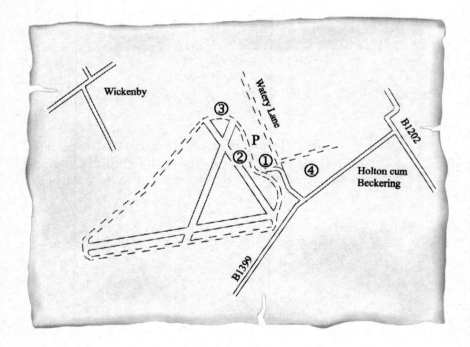

AT WAR

No 1 Group, Bomber Command. Operational 1942-45. First to arrive was 12 Squadron, flying Wellingtons and then Lancasters. This unit remained until flying ceased three years later and would suffer heavy losses. On 28/29 April 1943, for example, four of 12 Squadron's aircraft were lost during mine-laying operations off Heligoland. The crew of one of these (ED 408) included navigator Basil Veira. Born in

The old control tower at RAF Wickenby, still in use at what is now Wickenby Aerodrome - an airfield used by freight hauliers.

St. Kitts, Veira was one of many black RAF personnel flying both with bomber command and as fighter pilots. In November 1943, 626 Squadron arrived and the demanding bombing schedule continued. Both Wickenby squadrons participated in 'Operation Hurricane', subjecting Germany's industrial heartland to 24-hour bombing on 14 October 1944. Flying continued into the autumn of 1945 when 12 Squadron moved to RAF Binbrook and 626 Squadron was disbanded.

IN PEACE

For ten years after the war, the RAF used Wickenby for storage, after which much of the land was returned to agriculture. In the 1960s, light aircraft began to use the northern portion of the airfield. Today, although some light industry occupies the site, Wickenby is a busy recreational airfield and the children's charity, 'Flights for Life' is based here.

159

FEATURES OF INTEREST

Control Tower with museum (1).
Airfield Memorial (2).
T2 hangar (3).
Domestic sites (4).

EXPLORATION

As flying takes place here, movement is necessarily restricted. However, the Holton cum Beckering-Snelland road runs through the main airfield site, and a bridle track, Watery Lane, facilitates exploration of the domestic sites to the east.

TRIVIA

Bomber crews carried a homing pigeon so that if they had to take to the sea in a dinghy, the bird could be despatched with details of their location attached to its leg. Following an attack on Bochun on the Ruhr on 13/14 May 1943, a Wickenby Lancaster ditched in the North Sea. Five days later, thanks to this method of communication, the crew were picked up by a minesweeper.

CHECK OUT

RAF Wickenby Memorial Collection website.

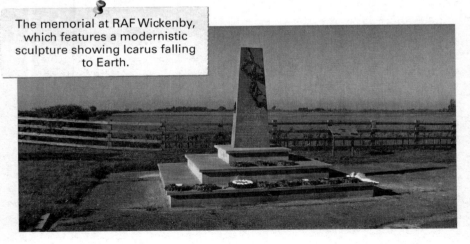

The memorial at RAF Wickenby, which features a modernistic sculpture showing Icarus falling to Earth.

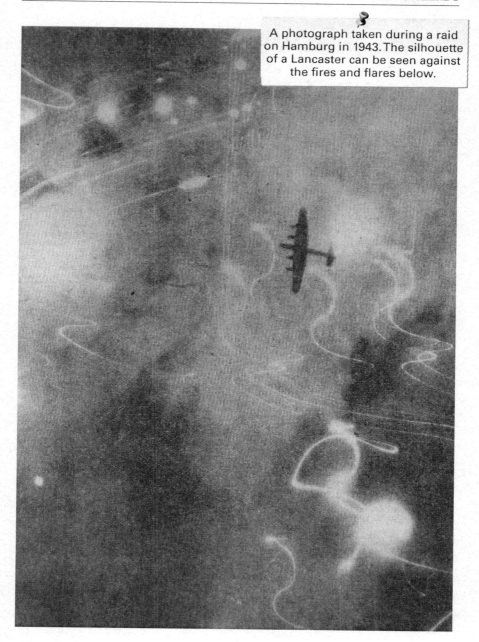

A photograph taken during a raid on Hamburg in 1943. The silhouette of a Lancaster can be seen against the fires and flares below.

40. RAF Woodhall Spa

Location: On the B1192, 5 miles north of Tattershall and Coningsby.
Car Parking: Thorpe Camp (P)/Ostler's Plantation/Woodhall Spa public car parks.
Map: OS Explorers 273 (2061).
Refreshments: The Bluebell Inn, Tattershall Thorpe and/or The Petwood, Woodhall Spa.

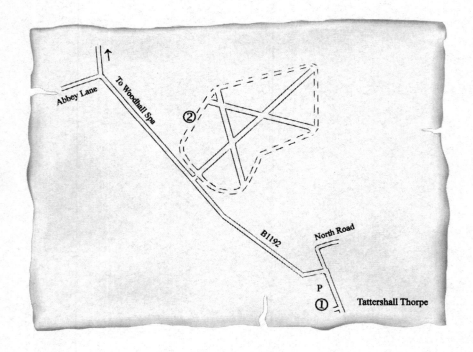

AT WAR
Group 5 Bomber Command. Operational 1942-45. Best known for its association with 617 Squadron which arrived at the beginning of 1944. On 8 September 1944, C.O. Wing-Commander Leonard Cheshire, was awarded the V.C. in recognition of his sterling service. Just eleven days later, on 19 September, 617's first C.O., Guy Gibson, took off from

The memorial at Woodhall Spa takes the form of a Lancaster propeller. It stands outside a visitor centre and museum.

Woodhall Spa to participate in a raid on the towns of Rheydt and Monchengladbach. His Mosquito crashed to the south of Rotterdam, at Steebergen, killing both Gibson and his navigator.

IN PEACE

Closed in 1945 and re-opened in 1960 as a Bloodhound missile base, after which a small enclave was retained by RAF Coningsby for use as a service depot. In 2003, the facility was mothballed. Cemex UK have used the remainder of the main airfield site for sand and gravel extraction, but Lincolnshire Wildlife Trust have bought the land to create a nature reserve. Thorpe Camp Visitor Centre, constructed around one of the domestic sites, is a museum concerned primarily with preserving the history of the base.

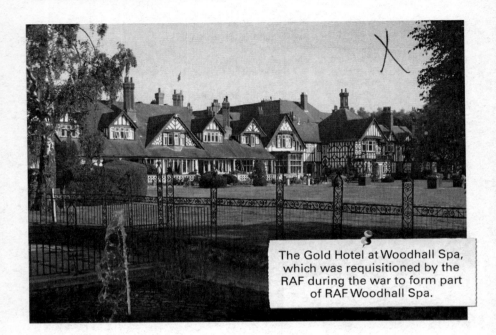

The Gold Hotel at Woodhall Spa, which was requisitioned by the RAF during the war to form part of RAF Woodhall Spa.

FEATURES OF INTEREST
Dambuster & 617 Squadron Memorials (Royal Square, Woodhall Spa).
Thorpe Camp Visitor Centre (1) (Entry Fee).
The Bluebell Inn (with memorabilia), near Visitor Centre on B1192.
The Petwood (with 617 Squadron memorabilia), Stixwould Road, Woodhall Spa.
617 Squadron plaque in St. Peter's Church, Woodhall Spa.
T2 hangar in RAF Woodhall enclave (2).

EXPLORATION
Domestic sites were distributed to the south east of the main airfield site. Further wartime structures are scattered about, notably off North Road and in Ostler's Plantation (accessible via Kirkby Lane, Woodhall Spa).

TRIVIA

Now a hotel, 'Petwood' was one of a number of Lincolnshire mansions taken over by the RAF. Built in 1905 for Lady Weighall, heiress of Sir Blundell Maple (of furniture store fame), it served in two world wars: as a convalescent home during the First World War and as Officers' Mess for RAF Woodhall Spa in the Second World War.

CHECK OUT

Thorpe Camp Visitor Centre website.

The Dambusters Memorial in the centre of Woodhall Spa commemorates those who lost their lives on the famous 1943 raid and is in the shape of a deluge of water breaching a dam.

A veteren's group meeting 50 years after the end of the war.

Bibliography

Ron Blake, Mike Hodgson & Bill Taylor, The Airfields of Lincolnshire Since 1912, Midland Counties, 1984.

Roger A. Freeman, Bases of Bomber Command Then and Now, Battle of Britain International Ltd., 2001.

Roger A. Freeman, UK Airfields of the Ninth Then and Now, After the Battle, 1993.

Bruce Barrymore Halpenny, Action Stations: Military Airfields of Lincolnshire and the East Midlands, Patrick Stephens Ltd., 1981.

Bruce Barrymore Halpenny, Ghost Stations: Lincolnshire, L'Aquila Publishing, 2008.

Terry Hancock, Bomber County, Midland Publishing, 2004.

Rupert Matthews, Heroes of Bomber Command: Lincolnshire, Countryside Books, 2005.

Martin Middlebrook & Chris Everett, The Bomber Command War Diaries, Viking, 1985.

Patrick Otter, Lincolnshire Airfields of the Second World War, Countryside Books, 1996.

General Websites of Interest

Airfields of Britain Conservation Trust
The Airfield Information Exchange
Bomber County Aviation Resource
Visit Lincolnshire Aviation
Lincolnshire Aviation Society

Addendum

The following sites, while not included within the main text, should not be ignored.

(1) RAF CAISTOR

Between Caistor and North Kelsey. OS Explorer 281 (0802). Relief Landing Ground for several stations 1940-45. Thor Missile base 1958-63. Little to see.

(2) RAF DONNA NOOK

Off the A1031, to the north of North Somercoates. OS Explorer 283 (4398). Relief Landing Ground for RAF North Coates 1940-45. Little to see. Currently (2014) a nature reserve and bombing range.

(3) RAF HARLAXTON

To the rear of Harlaxton Manor, adjacent to Harlaxton village. OS Explorer 247 (9032). A First World War airfield, brought back into service as Relief Landing Ground for RAF Grantham 1942-45. Little to see. The imposing Harlaxtion Manor was used as the officers' mess. See Heritage Lincolnshire website for details of open days.

(4) RAF MANBY

To the east of Louth, off the B1200. OS Explorer 283 (3886). Developed in the 1930s for armaments training. Continued in this role throughout the war years and beyond. Closed in 1974. Much of the airfield is now given over to agriculture, but many of the original structures survive within a business park setting. An ideal choice of location for starting to find your own way around an old airfield site.

(5) RAF STURGATE

To the east of Gainsborough, adjacent to the village of Upton. OS Explorer 271 (8787). Relief Landing Ground for RAF Blyton 1944-45. Used by USAF as a reserve airfield 1953-64. A portion of runway and the Control Tower (utilised by Lincoln Aero Club) remains.